As humanity's collect
more of us are exp
else hears, visions no one else sees, intense intuitive feelings
that presage the future or enable us to telepathically connect to
loved ones. Some of us communicate with the dead, see interdimensional beings, claim to have been abducted by aliens. And
some of us experience synchronicities that defy the odds.

Are we outliers?

Or are we, as a growing number of psychiatrists, scientists, and researchers now recognize, tapping into a matrix of
reality far more vast and complex than what science currently
recognizes?

PHENOMENA

HARNESSING YOUR PSYCHIC POWERS

BY ROB & TRISH MACGREGOR

For Megan,
with love bigger than Google
And our deepest thanks to the people who shared their experiences
with us

CONTENTS

INTRODUCTION

Some of us experience phenomena—voices no one else hears, visions no one else sees, intense, intuitive feelings that presage the future or enable us to telepathically connect to loved ones. Some of us communicate with the dead, see UFOs, claim to have been abducted by aliens. Some of us experience synchronicities that defy the odds.

Mainstream scientists who study the brain and human behavior often refer to these experiences as hallucinations or simply cases of misidentification. However, a growing number of psychiatrists, scientists and researchers now recognize that people who experience such phenomena may be tapping into a matrix of reality far more vast and complex than what science currently recognizes.

One of those scientists is British biologist Rupert Sheldrake, who has conducted experiments into psychic abilities for decades in spite of repeated attacks on his findings.

Telepathy

When you Google telepathy, one of the first links that comes up is a dictionary definition: the supposed communication of thoughts or ideas by means other than the known senses; mind-reading; thought transference. Notice the supposed? It's a subtle way of telling you that telepathy hasn't been proven scientifically, which simply isn't true.

The problem is that the consensus among mainstream scientists is that studies of telepathy and all psychic abilities are pseudoscience, fringe stuff. When Sheldrake published his experimental findings in peer-reviewed scientific journals, mainstream scientists and skeptics attacked his methodology, insulted him personally, and the science journal *Nature* even suggested in an editorial that his books should be burned.

In 2013, Sheldrake was invited to talk about his new book, *Science Set Free*, at a TEDx White Chapel event. Afterward, an anonymous panel of scientists working for TEDx determined that his talk should be banned because his theories crossed into pseudoscience. So the talk was banned, which ultimately provided Sheldrake and his ideas far more exposure and recognition than if the panel had simply ignored him. The talk can be found on YouTube and it's fascinating.

In his book, *The Sense of Being Stared At*, Sheldrake lays out his evidence for the existence of telepathy. From his scientific tests on telephone telepathy to the sense of being stared at to his research into the telepathy between people and their beloved pets, his case for telepathy is compelling.

His telephone experiment involved one individual and two to four callers. In a test run with three callers, there were 2,080 trials. In this test, a caller selects three people with whom they have a social bond. The monitor of the test uses a random number generator or a die roll to choose one of the three callers. That caller is then selected to call the participant. Before the phone is picked up, the participant is asked to choose which of the callers he or she thinks it is. The results were impressive. On average, participants guessed the caller 41.8%, considerably above the chance rate of 33.3 %.

"Seemingly telepathic experiences with telephones are very common," Sheldrake writes in *The Sense of Being Stared At*. "Indeed, they may be the commonest kind of telepathic experience in the modern world." He notes that the "evolution of telepathy" is ongoing and that email telepathy is the second most common type. "People find that they think of someone they have not thought about for a while, and shortly afterward receive an email from that person."

Telepathy is also common among parents and their children, people and their pets, close friends, married couples, and identical twins. Our neighbor, Annette, has an identical twin, Jannette. Over the years, they've experienced some dramatic instances of telepathy.

Some years ago, Jannette was living in Memphis with the man

she was dating at the time. She worked for Chanel, so numerous bottles of perfume lined her bathroom shelves. One night, a loud crash from the bathroom awakened her and her boyfriend. "Someone's broken into the house, they're in the bathroom," she whispered.

Her boyfriend grabbed a baseball bat and moved quickly and silently toward the bathroom, Janette right behind him. No intruder. But every bottle had fallen from the shelves and shattered against the floor, almost as if someone had swept an arm across the shelves, knocking them down. "Right then, I knew something had happened to Annette. I just knew it."

Moments later, the phone rang. It was Annette, who lived in another city, and she was hysterical, sobbing. She had just been robbed at gunpoint while delivering a night deposit to the bank for her employer. "While it was happening," Annette recalls, "I was praying that the guy wouldn't kill me. I was telling God that if I was killed, Jannette wouldn't survive it. My husband would, he would get past it, but Jannette wouldn't. I called her before I even called the police."

We asked how the bottles had gotten broken. She didn't know. The incident was an example of synchronicity, telepathy and—what else? Psychokinesis? But by what?

EVOLUTION OF THE PARANORMAL

Sixty years ago, back in the days of *Ozzie & Harriet*, the paranormal didn't play much of a role in popular culture. Typically, it was relegated to obscure magazines and journals or to TV shows like Rod Serling's *The Twilight Zone* (1959 to 1964) or to sci-fi movies like *The Village of the Damned* (1960). You didn't talk about this paranormal stuff in public.

When we met in 1981, we were both avid readers of the Seth books by Jane Roberts, which began with *Seth Speaks*, published in 1972. Seth was a non-physical entity channeled by Roberts and witnessed by her husband, Rob, who took copious notes of every session. Neither of us knew anyone who read these kinds of books or even had an interest in the subject matter. Our interest in and search for such phenomena became our common denominator.

FAST FORWARD TO THE CURRENT CENTURY.

In October 2017, Chapman University conducted a survey of "American fears" that included a battery of items on paranormal beliefs. These ranged from a belief in Bigfoot to psychic powers and haunted houses, ancient civilizations like Atlantis, to visits by aliens. The results show just how dramatically beliefs about the paranormal have changed: 55 percent believe that advanced civilizations like Atlantis existed; 52 percent believe places can be haunted by spirits; more than a third believe aliens visited Earth in the ancient past; more than a quarter believe aliens have visited the planet in modern times; and a quarter believe objects can be moved with the mind. The study concluded that 75 percent of Americans believe in some facet of the paranormal.

What's astonishing about this statistic is how it compares to a study conducted by Baylor University twelve years earlier, which concluded that just 15 percent of Americans believed in the paranormal. What accounts for the increase? How were the studies conducted? Did the phrasing of the questions account for some of the differences in the statistics? Even when taking such qualifiers into account, the Chapman study shows a dramatic increase in interest in the paranormal.

Ironically, this boost in curiosity about such mysterious matters might be related to technology—specifically, social media. Numerous websites, blogs, Twitter, Facebook and Instagram interest groups that focus on psychic phenomena have had a tremendous impact. It also could be the result of a proliferation of movies and TV shows about different facets of the paranormal. Then there are books, workshops, and seminars, an entire cottage industry that has grown up in the last twenty years and revolves around the human curiosity about and need for expanded awareness.

Scientists on the cutting edge believe the old paradigm—that our perception is limited to the five senses—is changing. But ordinary people have long experienced paranormal phenomena and their stories tell us that a paradigm shift has been underway for years. Only now is it reaching a tipping point.

ORDINARY PEOPLE

When artist Renie Wiley was a young girl growing up in South Florida, she used to have visions about future events and thought that everyone had such abilities. Then one day in grade school she had a vision and blurted out what she was seeing. She told the teacher that her car was going to get a flat tire. The next day at her lunch break, the teacher walked out to her car and discovered a flat tire, just as Renie had predicted. She accused the girl of deflating her tire, sent her to the principal's office, and her parents were called in. Renie was suspended from school for several days and it was a long time before she ever again revealed any of her visions.

Renie quietly nurtured her ability over the years, grew into it, accepted it, and eventually worked with South Florida police departments in finding missing children.

Part of the resistance to anomalous phenomena is the result of religious beliefs as well as the posture of mainstream science that largely dismisses the paranormal as nonsense believed by ignorant and gullible people. Even though the weirdness factor isn't as pervasive in this century as it was decades ago, it still prevents some people from talking openly about their experiences.

When Leiny Krumm was a child growing up in Colombia, she woke one night to see her recently deceased grandmother standing at the foot of her bed. She wasn't afraid, just startled, and sat up and started talking with her. It happened frequently in her childhood and Leiny's mistake was telling her parents, strict Catholics, that her *abuelita* had been visiting her. They hired a priest to perform an exorcism on their home, with special attention on Leiny's bedroom and on Leiny herself.

Today, she's a mother of two in her early forties and still sees spirits and hears voices. The voices are most prevalent when she meditates and they offer guidance and advice. Her grandmother's visits aren't as frequent as they were when she was a kid, but Leiny still sees her occasionally and is comforted by her presence. "It's just part of who I am," she says. "I've accepted it, even if my parents haven't."

Leiny's husband is well aware of her predisposition to hear voices and see things that other people generally don't see. But they don't talk much about it and it isn't something Leiny readily reveals about herself. She knows other people might not believe her experiences are real or might view them in a negative way.

Renie's teacher may have considered her outburst inappropriate, but how did that warrant the principal's office and suspension? Did the teacher perhaps believe that no one can see the future? Was that the real issue? Leiny's Catholic parents believed her experiences indicated something evil had entered their daughter's life and felt it was their duty to call in a priest to help them deal with it.

FEAR IS A POWERFUL INHIBITOR.

Even though such phenomena can be symptomatic of mental disorders, they can also be the manifestation of an individual's intuitive and psychic abilities, including mediumship. These kinds of abilities may still remain beyond the borders defined by mainstream science, but not as strenuously as decades ago. Part of this progress is due to evolving technology.

In Dawson Church's book *Mind to Matter: The Astonishing Science of How Your Brain Creates Material Reality*, the author notes that "Modern neuroscience...gives us the ability to map the neural signaling involved in consciousness and describe the signaling pathways active in the emotional brain."

When altered states occur—through meditation, psychic experiences, or feelings of ecstasy—an EEG "records large amplitudes of alpha, theta, and delta simultaneously." When physical healing takes place in this altered state, "flares of theta are usually evident," Church writes.

He's referring to brain waves and how they change during altered states. These changes alter our physical reality in some way—a physical or emotional healing, a release of stress, worry, anxiety, increased immunity, greater happiness. "Matter is changed by mind," Church contends.

So change is occurring, but perhaps not as quickly as we would like. It's why phenomena we experience are often dismissed as anomalies. By definition, an anomaly is an outlier, something that doesn't fit with the accepted mold, the standard. The term comes from the Greek word *anomolia*, meaning "uneven" or "irregular."

Traditional cultures still connected with humanity's pre-technological, pagan past consider paranormal experiences and phenomena not only as normal, but as events of greater significance. We'll explore cultural differences and their beliefs about phenomena in depth.

CREATIVITY & PHENOMENA

Creativity often serves as a conduit to experiencing phenomena. When M. Night Shyamalan was attempting to come up with an idea for a movie script, he had a vision of a young boy at a gathering after a funeral, standing on a stairway talking to no one. Then he realized the boy was talking to the spirit of the dead person.

That scene was the start of *The Sixth Sense*, a movie that captivated audiences and catapulted Shyamalan to fame. So essentially, as Shyamalan explained to Britt Hayes in an interview for *Screencrush*, a vision of his own instigated a story about a boy's visions. Cole Sear—played by Haley Joel Osment—sees ghosts and is terrified by his visions. He can't tell anyone else about what he sees, not even his mother. But then he meets a child psychologist, Dr. Malcolm Crowe—played by Bruce Willis—who not only believes him, but is (spoiler alert) actually dead.

Novelists often experience phenomena about their characters—visions, voices, dreams, telepathy—where the personality of the character comes through so loudly and clearly, it's as if you're sitting across the table from them. For Stephen King, the idea for *Dreamcatcher* came to him through a series of dreams in 1999 while he was recuperating after being hit by a car. In an interview with *SFGate* in 2003, he said the first idea that occurred to him after the accident was four guys in a cabin in the woods. "Then you introduce one guy who staggers into camp saying, 'I don't feel well,' and he brings this awful hitchhiker with him. I dreamed a lot about that cabin and those guys in it."

Paranormal phenomena that hold personal messages, as King describes, can come through the dreamstate and include hypnagogic and hypnopompic images that we see or hear as we're falling asleep or waking up. Mary Shelley's idea for *Frankenstein* came to her in a vivid vision she described in the introduction to her novel, where she saw "the pale student of unhallowed arts kneeling beside the thing he had put together." The student had tried "to mock the stupendous mechanism of the Creator of the world" by giving the "spark of life" to a "hideous corpse."

Our daughter, Megan, is an artist whose paintings of animals began with an internship at Disney World's Epcot Center, where she worked with dolphins. She paints from photographs, but because she has such an unusual eye for color, the image moves well beyond the photo. "Once I begin painting, certain colors speak to me and I see those colors in my head."

Over the centuries, many famed artists—da Vinci, van Gogh, M.C. Escher, Michelangelo, and Picasso among them—have created from their visions. Where did Mona Lisa's enigmatic smile really originate? What gave birth to van Gogh's *Starry Night*? Or to M.C. Escher's *Metamorphosis I* and *II*? Is the starting point for all creativity what Stephen King calls "dreaming awake?"

THE HOLOGRAM

If we live within a matrix where everything unfolds from the inside out, as writer Michael Talbot discusses in his classic book *The Holographic Universe*, then paranormal phenomena are part of our DNA, our heritage as spiritual beings alive in a physical universe. This heritage includes both common and bizarre psychic experiences. From telepathy to ghosts and haunted houses, from clairvoyance, precognition, and synchronicity, to contact with the dead and UFOs and aliens, it all falls under the umbrella of *phenomena*.

Maybe by experiencing such phenomena the collective consciousness of humanity expands, leaps beyond itself, and propels us into an exploration of this emerging new paradigm.

That strikes us as a journey worth taking.

1

SEEING THINGS

"Vision is the art of seeing what is invisible to others."
Jonathan Swift

Late one afternoon in June 2000, Rob was sitting at his desk, trying to work on a manuscript, but felt worn out and exhausted from our move several days earlier. The move had been only fifteen miles, from a three-bedroom house where we'd lived since our daughter was six weeks old. Trish's dad had moved in with us a year earlier, when her mother had been committed to an Alzheimer's unit, and Megan had given him her bedroom and had been sleeping in the living room. The new house had five bedrooms and was large enough for everyone to have a room.

Trish was in the kitchen, about to leave for the nursing home where her mother was going to be transferred into hospice and Rob, still in his office, briefly shut his aching eyes and massaged them with his fingers. He suddenly saw Trish's mother, smiling, animated, waving at him, then she turned and walked away. He didn't have any idea what, if anything, it meant, and didn't have a chance to think about it because less than a minute later, the phone rang, startling him.

It was the nursing home, calling Trish to let her know her mother had just died.

Rob understood he'd just had a vision of her waving good-bye.

Visions, like voices, come in many shapes and forms and have any number of triggers. They can occur during hypnagogic sleep, which we experience shortly before we fall asleep. Visions are also induced in altered states like meditation, relaxation, sensory deprivation, imagination, drugs, a high fever, alcohol withdrawal, migraines, rituals, any transcendent state, and through dreams.

Rob's vision of Trish's mother occurred in a kind of hypnagogic state. Sometimes the visions in this state seem to be random, nonsensical, a mishmash of emotions, events, and images from the day. But then there are times when we see something so specific it might kick us into full consciousness and we recall the vision. That was what happened to Rob when he saw Trish's mother wave good-bye.

This same relaxed state is what we experience during meditation. The reasoning left-brain is quieted to the point where the right-brain is able to hear and see what lies beyond our normal senses.

In 2010, Rob taught a meditation course at a local gym. During the July 12 class, he directed us to a point in the future where we could hear or see a headline—in a newspaper, on TV, the radio, the Internet. He instructed us to see it vividly, with captions and photos.

At the time, the Deepwater Horizon oil spill was in its third month. It had begun on April 20 in the Gulf of Mexico, when a BP oil rig exploded in the gulf, just fifty miles off the Louisiana coast, killing eleven people and injuring seventeen. At the time, it was considered to be the worst oil spill in history, with more than 200 million gallons of crude oil pumped into the gulf for a total of eighty-seven days before it was capped. On the day of the meditation class, the leak was capped and the looming question in the news was whether the cap would hold.

Rob's soothing voice took Trish to the border of sleep and as she was perched there, she saw the new containment cap working. The gusher of oil either slowed or stopped. But she dismissed it as wishful thinking and then promptly zoned out. When Rob brought the class out of meditation, he went around the room, asking everyone what they'd seen.

One woman said she had seen the new containment cap working, the same thing Trish had seen. Rob said he had seen rectangular shapes that were yellow, against a kind of purple background, scenes that later appeared on the news. On September 19, the well was officially declared to be dead.

Oliver Sacks, a British neurologist and author of *Hallucinations*, called these types of visions "inner hallucinations" because they aren't projected into external space but are seen on the inside of your eyelids. They typically occur, Sacks writes in near-sleep states, with the eyes closed. But these inner hallucinations still have all the characteristics of hallucinations: "They are involuntary, uncontrollable, and may have preternatural color and details or bizarre forms and transformations, quiet unlike normal visual imagery."

THE EMOTIONAL COMPONENT

With some, if not most visions, there's an important emotional component. For months, most of us had seen heartbreaking photos and videos of the oil spill, of the affected wildlife covered in black sludge, struggling to survive, and had heard the dire predictions by oceanographers and other scientists about the long-term effects of the spill. So the spill was on everyone's mind and there was a collective, global anxiety about it. It's not surprising then that several of us in the class had seen something about it.

Emotions certainly played into a vivid vision Trish experienced the night after our daughter, Megan, was born. The night nurse had just taken her back to the nursery after her feeding and Trish settled back down in her bed, in the ward she shared with three other women. As she drifted off toward sleep, she suddenly heard her name being called. She sat up and looked around the ward, certain one of the other women was awake and had called out to her. But the other three women were sound asleep and the door to the ward was shut. She figured she had imagined it.

She laid back down once more and when she heard her name again, realized that although the female voice seemed to be external to her, she was hearing it internally. So she shut her eyes and silently invited whoever this was to identify herself.

A vision exploded across the inner screen of her eyes of a young woman she felt was Megan. She was perhaps forty, so that would put the date around 2029, and Trish had the impression she was in the midst of a hypnotic regression in an attempt to find out certain information about her early life. She lived in a vastly changed world where rising oceans and other natural disasters had reshaped the country, destroyed records, and left gaping holes in her knowledge of her early life.

Trish provided her the information she requested—where we lived at the time she was born, her birth data, what books we were writing in those early years, the texture of our lives. Megan thanked Trish and the vision went dry.

In retrospect thirty years later, we wonder if the vision was of a granddaughter rather than of Megan. But then again, back in 1989, Al Gore's An Inconvenient Truth wouldn't be released for another seventeen years and the words "climate change" and "global warning" were not part of the lexicon, except, perhaps, among a small group of scientists. The only template for the kind of devastation Trish's vision offered of Megan's world came from Edgar Cayce, the most documented psychic of the twentieth century.

In this reading, Cayce may have been addressing the breaking up in 2017 of the Larsen C ice shelf in the Antarctica, a section of ice nearly the size of Delaware.

"As to the changes physical again: The earth will be broken up in the western portion of America. The greater portion of Japan must go into the sea. The upper portion of Europe will be changed as in the twinkling of an eye. Land will appear off the east coast of America. There will be the upheavals in the Arctic and in the Antarctic that will make for the eruption of volcanoes in the torrid areas, and there will be the shifting then of the poles—so that where there has been those of a frigid or the semi-tropical will become the more tropical, and moss and fern will grow. And these will begin in those periods in '58 to '98…"—January 19, 1934

Cayce made a lot of Earth-change predictions, but his dates weren't correct, which leads skeptics to contend that none of his material is valid. But in our experience, psychics are rarely correct about the timing of events. They see patterns of possibility, then try to pinpoint those possibilities in time—six months, a year, three years or fifty—and often fail utterly and miserably. What *is* valid is what we experience in our own lives. This vision thirty years ago of Megan and her world was so real that throughout Megan's childhood, we made sure she was provided with the information she had requested.

DRUGS

Since the 1960s when hallucinogenics came into play in American culture in such a major way, drug-induced visions became fairly commonplace. But the methods and experiences differed vastly. Author and researcher Terrence McKenna took peyote, talked to mushrooms, and unlocked what may be a key to the *I Ching*, a Chinese divination system that dates back more than 5,000 years.

Carlos Castaneda took peyote when he was an anthropology student at UC Berkeley, met Don Juan, a shaman who may or may not have been real, and wrote his doctoral dissertation about the experience. *The Teachings of Don Juan* and subsequent books have sold millions of copies and launched a popular interest in shamanism.

In May 1953, Aldous Huxley took mescaline under the supervision of British psychiatrist Humphry Osmond, who had spent the previous year researching the use of mescaline in schizophrenics in a mental hospital in Saskatchewan. One of Huxley's most famous books, *The Doors of Perception* describes his experience with mescaline that May afternoon and was published a year later. On college campuses in the Sixties, the book was widely read and considered to be a kind of map to transcendence.

Mescaline and its more controversial sibling, LSD, were the favored psychedelics in the Sixties and allowed experiencers to enter a world Huxley described when he looked at a simple vase of flowers. "I was not looking now at an unusual flower arrangement. I was seeing what Adam had seen on the morning of his creation—the miracle, moment by moment, of naked existence."

The promise of what Huxley described so eloquently resulted in a psychedelic explosion. "...transience that was yet eternal life, a perpetual perishing that was at the same time pure Being, a bundle of minute, unique particulars in which, by some unspeakable and yet self-evident paradox was to be seen the divine source of all existence."

When Oliver Sacks read Huxley's *Doors of Perception* and *Heaven and Hell*, he was "especially excited by his speaking of the 'geography' of the imagination and its ultimate realm—'the Antipodes of the mind.'"

An antipode is defined as something diametrically opposed to something else. But both Huxley and Sacks were referring to "regions of the mind" that allow a person to be conscious of things that wouldn't usually concern him because they don't have anything to do with his typical concerns in the external world. "Like the earth of a hundred years ago, our mind still has its darkest Africas, its unmapped Borneos and Amazonian basins," Huxley wrote in *Heaven and Hell*. And in these unmapped places inside of us, we'll encounter all sort of strange creatures. "You do not invent these creatures... They live their own lives in complete independence. A man cannot control them."

But these unmapped areas of the mind can be experienced through mescaline and hypnosis. The visions that result are unique to each of us and yet share certain characteristics.

HYPNOSIS

In the late 1980s, we had the good fortune of knowing several Fort Lauderdale area psychics—all of them now deceased. One evening, we were at Tony Grosso's home in nearby Pembroke Pines. Tony, a short, stout man, often worked as a psychic on cruise ships. He was flamboyant and eccentric and a powerful empath. Tony had a unique system for his readings that involved color and he and Rob eventually co-authored a book on color divination, *The Rainbow Oracle*.

Also with us was Renie Wiley, who had worked as a psychic consultant with local cops and was the subject of an article on psychic detectives that we wrote for *Fate Magazine*. On that particular evening, we were just four people intrigued by what the future might hold for us—as individuals, as a human collective. Renie suggested that she hypnotically progress us into the future to see if we could pick up anything on what life would be like.

Renie thought the progression should be to "an undetermined future," and felt we would see what we needed to see. She had a beautiful voice, soft, hypnotic, and as she spoke, Trish suddenly saw herself as a very tall, bald woman, living in a dome because the external world was so toxic. Life in the dome wasn't exactly a panacea—bureaucracy abounded and there were constant threats from the external environment, violent storms that often weakened the dome walls. Other factions of humanity lived in nearby caverns and their lives had evolved quite differently.

The dome scenario was confirmed a couple years after that progression when we discovered a book by Chet Snow and Helen Wambach, *Mass Dreams of the Future*. Wambach, a psychologist, had progressed 2,500 individuals in Europe to the year 2100 and asked them to describe what their lives were like. In all three scenarios that emerged, the population of the planet was greatly reduced. In one scenario, survivors lived in huge domes that protected them from the air outside.

This progression always stuck with Trish. After the hurricane season of 2017—Harvey, Irma, and Maria, all either category 4s or 5s—and the quakes in Mexico and Japan and elsewhere, it all suggests that we're in the beginning throes of extreme climate change. It's the kind of climate change that drives people inland in droves because it's no longer safe to live on the coasts.

As Irma approached Florida as a category 5, with the early forecasts taking her up Florida's east coast, we decided we should evacuate to Atlanta, where Trish's sister lives. But gas was scarce and the idea of getting stranded on the interstate or turnpike was a deterrent. So we opted for a friend's place north of Orlando. We had enough gas to get there. But in the end, we decided to stay at home.

Friends who evacuated said it took eight hours to get to Orlando (a drive that usually takes about two and a half to three hours), and eighteen hours to reach southern Georgia. Cars ran out of gas on the turnpike and were abandoned. At one point, when Irma's winds reached 180 miles per hour, we figured we'd made a big mistake by not evacuating. The largest evacuation in Florida history—and perhaps in U.S. history—was underway. Fortunately for us, the center of the hurricane shifted to the Gulf of Mexico, sparing the east coast of Florida.

In August 2019, this same scenario was repeated with Hurricane Dorian. At one point, the National Hurricane Center had the category 5 hurricane coming straight into West Palm Beach. But the spaghetti models were all over the place. We put up hurricane shutters, stocked up on food and supplies, filled the cars with gas. Then on August 31, the day Dorian was supposed to come ashore, the hurricane stalled. On September 1, Dorian slammed into the Abaco Islands with maximum sustained winds of 185 mph, and stalled over the Abacos and Grand Bahama Island for forty hours. The Abacos were devastated, 70,000 people were left homeless, and most structures were destroyed. In West Palm Beach, we got a little rain and wind.

But these natural disasters, especially when they happen back to back, as Harvey and Irma did in 2017, the psychological and psychic toll it takes is considerable. Your body slams into survival mode. And for Trish, standing on the back porch during parts of Irma and listening to and seeing the wind and rain tear through our yard, and anxiously watching updates on Dorian two years later, that progression so many years before came to mind.

DREAM VISIONS

Sensing the future through dreams, the most common way to experience precognition, can often be more direct and accurate than visions or impressions that come through in altered states. When we dream, our logical minds slip into the background and our intuitive minds reach more easily through time and space. Just ask Ray Getzinger.

When he was twelve, he used to dream about a redheaded woman from Georgia who wore her hair in ringlets. A decade later, in 1966, he married a woman with red hair who lived in

Virginia and was born in Georgia. About a year after they'd been married, she began styling her hair in ringlets just as Ray had seen in his dream. Amazingly, he had never mentioned that dream to his wife.

The stunning part of this precognition isn't just the detail, but also the fact that the dream occurred ten years before Ray met that redhead from Georgia.

In 1845, Elias Howe was struggling to figure out how to automate his sewing process. When he fell asleep one night, he had a vivid nightmare that he'd been captured by savages who attacked him with spears that had eye-shaped holes at the end. When he woke up, he realized the dream had provided the final piece of the puzzle for his new sewing machine. The end of the needle needed an eye. This invention made Howe the second wealthiest person in the country and revolutionized the garment industry.

Howe had been deeply immersed in creative and imaginative work that consumed him. When he fell asleep, that creative intensity soared past his analytical left brain and tapped into what theoretical physicist F. David Peat called "the space between," in order to find a solution. Without that dream, Howe's sewing machine may been delayed for years or might not have happened at all.

Einstein experienced something similar. Thanks to a series of dreams he had as a young kid, he eventually came up with this theory of relativity. The dream itself was, well, weird.

He dreamed he was walking through a farm and came upon a herd of cows huddled together against an electric fence. When the farmer suddenly switched the fence on, Einstein saw all the cows jump back at the same time; they'd been shocked. He thought he'd witnessed some sort of synchronized cow behavior and told the farmer what he'd seen. But the farmer, who had been standing at the opposite end of the field, had seen something different. He'd seen the cows jump away one by one. Einstein couldn't dismiss the dream. And over the years, this dream led him to the theory that events look different depending on where you're standing because of the time it takes light to reach your eyes.

In March 2019, Rob dreamed that he and Trish were traveling somewhere and that their Golden Retriever, Noah, was with us. He was a large dog—105 pounds—but in the dream he was thin, and was following along behind us with Trish's dad, who had passed in 2005. The dream was unsettling.

At the time, Noah had been sick with what we thought was just an infection. But by mid-March, his blood work looked bad, he was anemic, lethargic, and not eating much. Our vet suspected he might have cancer and recommended an ultrasound, which would reveal more than the X-rays had.

The ultrasound indicated that the problem was his spleen, which was throwing off clots. The specialty vet recommended the removal of his spleen and immediate hospitalization. Noah was ten, there was no guarantee that removing his spleen would prolong his life, particularly if he had cancer. We asked the specialty vet to send our vet the ultrasound and test results and we would decide what to do by the next day.

Very early the next morning, Rob found Noah in the dining room, and ran in to wake Trish. "I think Noah is dying."

We hurriedly got ready to take him to the vet. But Noah weaved into the family room, barely able to walk, and climbed onto the couch. He lay down next to our other Golden, Nigel, and rested his head on his haunches. When we were ready to leave for the vet's office, he couldn't make it past the family room doorway. He passed peacefully, surrounded by people and animals who loved him.

The dream had proven to be accurate.

REMOTE VIEWERS

No book on phenomena—and specifically in a chapter on visions—would be complete without a nod toward the remote viewers, people who can see things or events taking place beyond the range of normal perception. The ability is also known as clairvoyance (literally "clear visions"), but the older term has been largely replaced by remote viewing in the decades since the U.S. Army secretly delved into "psychic spying."

From 1972 to 1995, more than $20 million was poured

into the government's psychic spy program, Stargate. The army and various intelligence agencies including the FBI, CIA, and DIA were involved. Most of the targets dealt with defense and national security issues and involved psychically spying on enemies. (You can find more on Stargate and read samples of remote viewing transcripts from actual sessions at remoteviewed.com.)

We had the good fortune of getting to know Joe McMoneagle. He was known as Remote Viewer #001 in the Stargate program, one of several names that was applied to the government's psychic spying program over its twenty-three-year existence. Joe joined the program in 1978 and remained until the end.

Trish initially became friends with Nancy (Scooter) McMoneagle, Joe's wife, through their mutual interest in astrology. Meanwhile, Rob had gotten to know Joe after he read the manuscript of Rob's remote viewing-related novel, *PSI/NET*, that was co-authored with actor Billy Dee Williams. That led us to a few traveling adventures with Joe and Scooter. One trip took us into the "Bermuda Triangle," where we were caught in a hurricane and trapped for days behind floodwaters on the island of Eleuthera. Since we live in hurricane territory in south Florida, we knew how to prepare with water, food that didn't require refrigeration, flashlights, and candles. We managed well—though ultimately we had to be rescued to get out—while others walked through waist-high water searching for food and fresh water.

After the Stargate program ended, McMoneagle began doing speaking engagements and offering private sessions. That led him to becoming a fixture on Japanese television where he starred in a psychic detective documentary series. We'll get more into psychic detectives in a later chapter, but here we'll briefly describe one of Joe's amazing feats in Japan.

While he wasn't always successful at finding missing people in Japan, in this case he was shockingly accurate. McMoneagle was given an envelope bearing a set of random numbers on the outside by one of the show's producers. Inside the envelope was the name of a forty-eight-year-old woman who had been missing for twenty-seven years. Without even opening the envelope, McMoneagle was able to remote view his target and give authorities the exact location of the woman, including the island, city, and specific prefecture (district) within the city. He described the apartment complex, the apartment building, picked the right floor and even directed authorities to a specific apartment. Japanese police and television crews were suitably impressed.

"They were very surprised to find her actually residing in it under her maiden name," McMoneagle wrote in an email. "I think it woke up the Japanese detective agency and police. I don't think they ever expected me to find her."

Skeptics often bring up all the times when psychics are wrong or inaccurate. It's true that focusing only on psychic successes might give the false impression that remote viewing and other psychic talents, *always* works. They don't.

Joe McMoneagle, like the rest of us, is clearly human and fallible. When we went with Joe and Scooter to Eleuthera, Trish kept saying that a storm in the North Atlantic was headed toward Eleuthera and would become a hurricane. Due to research for novels over the years, she had closely tracked hurricanes and didn't like the outlook. But Joe insisted it wasn't going to hit us. Then again, he wasn't remote viewing the storm. He was hoping for a sunny island vacation. He might be one of the world's best remote viewers, but he apparently can't change the weather!

We got hit, lost power and water for days, and played Scrabble by candlelight in the evenings.

2

HEARING THINGS

"Voices inside my head, echo the things that you said."
—The Police, "Voices Inside My Head"

Some people hear voices and consider them helpful, a means of guidance. They aren't frightened by them and don't consider them intrusive. In fact, they welcome the voices.

Jane Clifford, who lives in Wales, is one such individual. For the last forty years, she has described herself as a clairvoyant psychic and healer. She hears voices and it's always the same voice coming from inside her head. She calls it her intuitive voice; it lets her know about things coming up.

Several years ago, Jane and a friend planned to spend a week in Spain, staying with people they knew whose home was on a mountaintop. A guest room was already prepared for them. Her friend found an inexpensive flight and texted Jane that she could book them. "But I got a resounding NO, with no reason given." And because Jane follows the advice of this voice, she told her friend not to book the flight. The next day, her friend called to inform her that flash floods had washed the guest room down the mountain and that their visit would have to be delayed until September.

In March of 2011, the voice told her on three consecutive nights, "You are to go to Egypt." At the same time, a picture of King Tut's cobra headdress appeared in her mind's eye.

"I've never been big into Egyptian gods and myths, so it was a surprise." I laughed and replied to the voice: "If you find me a travel companion and somewhere to stay that's not in a crowded tourist hotel, I'll consider it." Within a week, a woman she'd recently met, Vanessa, asked Jane to spend a month in a Bedouin camp in Sinai with her. She accepted the offer and spent a fascinating month in Egypt.

Other people who hear voices just want to banish them. When these individuals seek medical help through traditional medicine, they often are treated with drugs that might silence the voices, but can cause a host of physical problems. Part of their challenge is that it's difficult to talk about their experiences because loved ones and friends may react negatively. That's why an organization was started decades ago to help people deal with the issue.

HEARING VOICES NETWORK

It's international in scope and advocates for people who hear voices. First formed thirty years ago, the Hearing Voices Network includes twenty nationally-based networks around the world. According to their website, the network incorporates "a fundamental belief that there are many ways to understand the experience of hearing voices and other unusual or extreme experiences."

The network begins with the premise that voices are real and meaningful, something experienced by a significant minority of people, including many who have no problems living with their voices. "Our research shows that to hear voices is not the consequence of a diseased brain, but more akin to a variation in human behavior, like being left-handed. It is not so much the voices that are the problem, but the difficulties that some people have in coping with them."

We first became aware of this organization through an article published on June 27, 2017 in *The Atlantic*—"Psychics Who Hear Voices Could Be On to Something". The author, Joseph Frankel, focuses on a psychic medium who was part of a study conducted by Philip Corlett and Albert Powers, a psychologist and psychiatrist at Yale. In a study they carried out, they compared "self-described psychics" who hear voices with people diagnosed with a psychotic disorder who experience auditory hallucinations.

Their conclusion is intriguing. They found similarities between the patients who heard psychic voices and patients who were diagnosed with a disorder, but with significant differences. The psychics were able to "control the onset and offset of their voices...were less distressed by their voice-hearing experiences." They also discovered that when the psychic voice hearers first admitted to hearing voices, their reception by others was more positive.

Patients, however, "were more likely to receive a negative reaction when sharing their voices with others for the first time, and this was subsequently more disruptive to their social relationships."

Corlett and Powers concluded that the group of healthy voice hearers "may have much to teach us about the neurobiology, cognitive psychology and ultimately the treatment of voices that are distressing."

PRACTICE: YOUR VOICES

We hope you're reading this book not only for information about phenomena, but also as a way of assessing your own abilities and experiences and looking for ways to understand them better, and possibly to expand upon them. So let's take an assessment of your perspective on voices.

How often do you hear voices?
Almost every day.
Occasionally.
Rarely.
Only when I'm falling asleep or waking up.
Never.
Are the voices positive?
Always
Most of the time
Sometimes
Never
Whether you hear voices or not, what is your opinion about the phenomena?
It's a problem, possibly a serious one.

I wish they would go away and leave me alone.

The voice I hear is helpful.

I talk to the voice and trust it.

I'm not sure if I've ever heard a voice in my head.

It's all imagination. I don't believe anyone hears voices that aren't their own thoughts.

What do you think is the source of voices that you or others hear?

It's definitely a part of me.

It's like a thought that comes out as a voice.

I don't know where it comes from. It's not me.

It's a part of me, but also separate.

I think some of these voices are communications from the other side.

If you hear voices, what would you like to know from the voice?

More about my future.

If you are part of me or separate.

When they will leave me alone.

How I can make more contact.

Keep your answers in mind as you read through the rest of this chapter. Or record them in a computer file or journal.

DRUGS VS. NO DRUGS

While mainstream psychiatrists might suggest drugs for patients who hear voices that repeatedly express negative sentiments, there's a growing trend—thanks largely to the Hearing Voices Network—to avoid medication and deal with the voices, even if they are antagonistic.

That was the case with R.W., whose interview with *STAT*, a health care newsletter, was published in July 2017. She'd been diagnosed with schizophrenia, had taken medications for more than a decade, and spent time in mental hospitals. Her voices, which came from three men, began when she was eighteen and told her she was stupid, that she should kill herself.

R.W. now accepts the voices as part of her life. She prefers to deal with them rather than try to bury them with drugs. Now she understands the voices as signals that she's feeling overwhelmed.

Many people in the international movement, like R.W., reject the idea that they are mentally ill, because they are not disturbed by the voices and are able to work and carry on a normal life. Dr. Dirk Corstens, a psychiatrist and psychotherapist in Maastricht in the Netherlands, is a leader in the movement. "For us, voices are a signal, they are something that tell you about your life. You have to listen to [them]. Not obey, but listen."

There are now more than 180 support groups worldwide, according to the Hearing Voices Network. Just how common is it to hear voices? A review of seventeen studies in nine countries, published in the *Journal of Mental Health*, concluded that about one in eight people hear voices.

CARL JUNG

The famed Swiss psychiatrist heard voices throughout his life. One of Jung's most stunning experiences began in early 1916 with a series of paranormal incidents in his home.

One Sunday afternoon around five PM, the front doorbell started ringing "frantically," Jung wrote in *Memories, Dreams, Reflections*. "Everyone immediately looked to see who was there, but there was no one in sight. I was sitting near the doorbell, and not heard it, but saw it moving. We all simply stared at one another. The atmosphere was thick, believe me!"

Jung knew something had to happen because the entire house felt as if it was crowded with spirits. "They were packed right up to the door and the air was so thick it was scarcely possible to breathe. As for myself, I was all aquiver with the question: 'For God's sake, what in the world is this?' Then they cried out in in chorus, 'We have come back from Jerusalem where we found not what we sought.' That is the beginning of the Septem Sermones."

The Seven Sermons to the Dead was written in a creative fever. In just three evenings, it was completed and "...the entire gathering of ghosts collapsed."

In Deirdre Bair's compelling biography, *Jung*, she writes that when *The Seven Sermons* is considered as a whole, it's a kind of "self-help textbook...for individuation and peaceful acceptance of the collective unconscious..."

In the winter of 1924, Jung spent long periods of time in solitude at the tower he'd built on the shores of Lake Zurich. For Jung, this tower, built entirely in stone and lacking modern amenities—like electricity or plumbing—was a "representation of individuation." Not surprisingly, he experienced voices and visions here. One evening, he was sitting by the fireplace and had a kettle heating on the fire to warm water so he could wash up. The water started boiling, the kettle whistled and sang, and suddenly, there seemed to be an orchestra inside the tower and another one outside. Jung sat and listened to this "concert" for more than an hour.

The music was soft, yet held all the "discords of nature." Jung felt this was right because nature isn't only harmonious, it is also "dreadfully contradictory and chaotic." He noted that the music was also like that. "...an outpouring of sounds, having the quality of water or wind—so strange it is simply impossible to describe it."

Jung, of course, treated patients who heard voices. One of the most interesting cases, which he talks about in his autobiography, was that of a schizophrenic older woman who heard voices "distributed throughout her entire body, and a voice in the middle of the thorax was 'God's voice,'" Jung writes.

He told her that was the voice they should rely on, because this particular voice made sensible remarks, and enabled him to manage this patient. One time the voice in the thorax, God's voice, told the woman to allow Jung to test her on the Bible. So for the next seven years, once every two weeks, Jung assigned her a chapter in the Bible to read and then tested her on it. "In this way," Jung wrote, "her attention was kept alert, so that she did not sink deeper into the disintegrating dream." After six years, the result of Jung's technique was that the voices that had once been everywhere throughout her body were now just on the left side. The right side was totally free of them. He concluded that she was cured, but only halfway.

Through his work with patients like this woman, he realized that paranoid ideas and hallucinations hold a kernel of meaning.

"A personality, a life history, a pattern of hopes and desires lie behind the psychosis.... At the bottom we discover nothing new and unknown in the mentally ill; rather, we encounter the substratum of our own natures."

It would be interesting if psychiatrists or psychologists conducted a study of mediums in the spiritualist town of Cassadaga, Florida, where most of the residents hear voices, communicate with the dead, and constantly are honing their skills.

CASSADAGA, FLORIDA

If you're headed out of Disney World east on I-4, the sign for Cassadaga is easy to miss unless you're paying attention. The tiny hamlet, tucked among hills—a rare phenomenon in Florida—exists in an alternate universe from the Orlando-area tourist theme parks. Whether you find the town or not may depend on how capricious the spirits are the day you visit.

On our first trip there in the early 1980s we got lost and stopped at a gas station in a nearby town and asked for directions. The long-haired young man, pumping gas into his battered pickup, studied us a few moments, then gave directions. As we thanked him and turned away, he said: "They talk to spooks there, you know."

"Yeah, we heard."

Established in 1894, Cassadaga may be the most unusual town in Florida. It's composed of two distinct areas. The actual spiritualist camp covers thirty-five acres and lies to the south of 430A, behind the Cassadaga Hotel. It's owned by the Southern Cassadaga Spiritualist Camp Meeting Association, which certifies the mediums who live and work in the camp.

Across the street from the camp, other mediums and psychics offer their services in shops and houses near the main road. They haven't been certified by the spiritualist association, so the implication is that they are opportunists, less skilled and talented than the certified mediums. Even in spiritual communities, bureaucracy abounds! And so do disagreements.

Cassadaga's mediums have a history of infighting over

rules and regulations as well as fending off practitioners who live outside the boundaries of the community. As in all small towns, gossip abounds...and you'll probably hear it if you stay around for a couple of days. It might be about the quality of readings of certain mediums or even whether or not ghosts occasionally encountered in the old hotel are friendly souls. The one we encountered on the second floor years ago was not!

We've visited Cassadaga many times over the years and have one friend who lives in the spiritualist community and one who lives outside it. Both are highly intuitive, hear voices and are successful, long-time practitioners, one of them a medium, the other a psychometrist who reads objects.

Mediumship, of course, knows no geographic boundaries, such as inside or outside of a spiritualist camp. Mediums act as an intermediary between the living and the dead, whether they have a certificate or not. Practicing mediums are clairaudient. In other words, they hear voices, and many of them also experience visions.

The Mediterranean-style hotel, built in the 1920s, dates back to the heyday of spiritualism, when the rich and the famous arrived for séances and readings. Along the right side of the hotel stretches a wide porch with picnic tables and rocking chairs. Sometimes in the evening, when the light plays tricks with perception, some of the empty chairs rock, creaking softly in the quiet. And your imagination slams into overdrive. Are there spirits in in those chairs, enjoying the evening?

Visitors meander along the narrow streets, passing old wood-framed houses with sloping front porches and white picket fences. Many of the houses feature hanging signs with the name of the resident medium, usually referred to as reverend. Spiritualist services are held on Sunday mornings in Colby Hall and whoever is leading the service usually does "spot" readings—selecting people from the attendees before the service ends.

FOLLOWING SENECA'S VOICE

The roots of Cassadaga go back to 1874 when, during a late

summer séance in Lake Mills, Iowa, George Colby, a twenty-seven-year-old medium from Pike, New York, heard *a voice*—and not just any voice, but that of an Indian spirit named Seneca. According to some, Colby reportedly said that Seneca manifested in physical form and instructed him to immediately leave Iowa and make contact with T. D. Giddings, a medium in Eau Claire, Wisconsin.

The two men, according to Colby's account, were to conduct another séance through which Seneca would spiritually commune with them. When they did so, they entered a trancelike state and were told that, "A congress of spirits has selected Florida for the establishment of a great spiritualist center..." And Colby had been chosen to lead in its creation.

In a series of spiritual sessions that followed, Colby continued receiving directions—more voices!—from his spirit guide, Seneca. He was told that the proposed location of this new spiritual center would be "near Blue Springs, Florida, on high pine hills overlooking a chain of silvery lakes."

It wasn't long before Colby and the entire Giddings family headed for Florida. This decision, based only on voices these two men heard, shows a remarkable acceptance of the validity of what Colby experienced.

In Jung's case, he initially believed that the voices he heard while he wrote *Seven Sermons* were probably evidence of madness. But because it was *his* experience—and not that of a patient—he didn't block those voices and ultimately came to look at this period of his life as his confrontation with his personal unconscious. Both Jung and Colby controlled the voices they heard. That may be the most significant difference between a medium and a schizophrenic or someone suffering from psychosis.

Colby, Giddings and their families boarded a steamboat in Jacksonville, and on the night of November 1, 1875, landed at Blue Springs, then a remote settlement of a couple of clapboard structures on the shore of the St. Johns River. Because of limited accommodations at Blue Springs, the Colby party resided temporarily in palmetto huts and awaited further instructions from Seneca. Then, late one night in the faint light of a kerosene lamp, they were contacted by Seneca with orders to "Go east, to the outskirts of the village and find the seven hills, this will be the place."

Once again, the two men did what Seneca told them. The next morning, traveling by mule and wagon, they headed from Blue Springs along a rutted sandy road that cut eastward through palmettos and slash pines. Near the town of present-day Lake Helen, they found seven pine-covered hills and saw the silvery lakes mentioned by Seneca. Colby and Giddings agreed that this was the spot where they were to build a new spiritual center.

By 1895, Cassadaga was becoming a popular winter retreat for spiritualists. In the early 1900s, advertisements in northern newspapers invited mediums to permanently relocate to the growing spiritualist camp. In the 1920s, Cassadaga was a regular settlement and a center of spiritualism and the hotel was built to accommodate the increasing number of visitors and mediums. George Colby died on July 27, 1933, his spirit-guided vision of a new center for spiritualism a reality.

INGO SWANN

He was one of the most famous psychics in recent decades, and participated in numerous scientific/government research projects in the 1970s and '80s. He was also an artist and an author of several books on the paranormal. After graduating from college in 1955, he joined the Army and soon found himself stationed in Korea where he was assigned to the staff of the commander of all forces in the Pacific. While working in the dangerous demilitarized zone where random shots were frequently fired, he heard a voice one day that saved his life.

He was attending a meeting between the U.S. forces and both the South and North Koreans in a temporary building where he helped organize some aspects of the protocol. During those meetings, the protocol required all participants to sit in assigned seats and not to move from the seats until the meeting was over. "Each side was worried about the possibility of assassination, and any untoward move by anyone was more than just frowned upon," Swann wrote in *Your Nostradamus Factor: Accessing Your Innate Ability to See into the Future.*

Swann was seated in his assigned chair at the end of the second row of "observers" when the incident occurred. Only the principals were allowed to speak, but about five minutes into the meeting, he heard a voice behind him, which he described as "a high-volume command." The voice said, "Get up. Get up now."

He stood up and realized there was no one behind him. All eyes in the room turned toward him as the conversation stopped, and hands reached for their weapons. "At that moment there was, in quick succession, a pop, and a thung. A bullet ripped through the pre-fab wall and hit the back of the chair where I'd been sitting, striking right where my heart would have been if I had remained sitting." The incident abruptly ended the meeting and Swann was cleared of any wrongdoing in the ensuing investigation.

Years later in New York City, Swann was listening to music at high volume through headphones on his Walkman when he was again saved by a voice. He was walking to a grocery store and after checking for traffic, was about to step off a curb when a loud voice shouted above the music: "Stop!" He stopped in mid-stride and moved back about three inches from the curb to catch his balance.

At that moment, an unseen car whizzed by, striking the curb, and the impact knocked Swann off his feet. The speeding vehicle was followed by a police car, its light spinning. His abrupt action had saved his life. "Later, when I had recovered, I rewound the tape and listened to see if the word *Stop!* was there. It wasn't."

VOICES FROM LITERATURE

In the March 5, 2017 of *Business Insider, Australia*, the headline of an article on hearing voices caught our attention: A surprising percentage of people report hearing voices of characters in stories even when they aren't reading. In that article, writer Kevin Loria explored the results of a survey conducted by researchers at Durham University in the UK in partnership with the Edinburgh International Book Festival and *The Guardian*. He reported, "...almost a fifth of readers said they hear the voices or thoughts of characters in regular life even when they aren't reading the book, something the researchers call 'experiential crossing.'"

As Loria noted, "When a good book is in your head and you are thinking about the 'voices' involved, it seems logical that those voices would add new perspective to what you see around you. But the study does add weight to the idea that in our brains, even fictional characters can seem real."

The authors of this particular study found that the parts of the brain associated with hearing voices become active when people read dialogue. "This illustrates a power of literature that might be unique to the medium," wrote Loria.

When the first Harry Potter book was published in 1997, our daughter was eight years old, in third grade. The book was the rage in elementary school and she was eager to read it. So off we went to Barnes & Noble. When we got home, she stretched out on the living room couch and read for hours. From then until the second book came out, she periodically would blurt out sentences that Harry or Hermione had said. We once asked her how she could remember the dialogues.

"I hear them in my head."

Clearly, hearing voices isn't confined to psychics or people who are mentally ill. The ability may be a natural part of who we are as human beings, a facet of our consciousness that is emerging in many people. But because we've been so indoctrinated to believe it isn't normal, we are, at the very least, *suspicious* of such people. Instead, we should be engaging them.

PRACTICE: LISTENING IN

But hearing voices is not an endeavor limited to mediums and psychics. Let's say you've never heard a voice or it has only happened rarely, and you've dismissed it. But now you would like to explore this phenomena and see how that voice can provide guidance, like the voice that warned Ingo Swann on two occasions that saved his life.

Here's a safe method you can use to make contact. Make sure you're serious about trying this practice. Before you begin, come up with a specific question you would like answered. Be sure it's something important to you, but keep it simple. If your question is too complicated, you may have difficulty interpreting whatever you hear. In addition to your question, it's a good idea to say to yourself that you are only receptive to supportive and helpful messages.

Find a comfortable place to sit or lie down at a time when you won't be disturbed. Take a few deep breaths and relax with each exhalation. As you shift to gentle breathing, surround yourself with a white or silver light of protection. Know that only positive energy will be allowed to enter your awareness and any negative energy headed toward you will be turned away.

When you start drifting toward sleep, freeze your awareness at that drowsy level of consciousness, known as the hypnagogic state. One way of doing that is to say to yourself, *I'm awake and aware, awake and aware.* This level of consciousness is where you're likely to hear a voice answering your question.

Write down whatever comes to you so you don't forget. Your answer may be indirect or symbolic, so you'll need to interpret the words as if they are part of a foreign language. For example, if you hear the name of an animal, what does that animal mean to you and how would that relate to your question?

If you hear any voices or you fall asleep, try again another time. If you keep trying, you'll hear a voice. Be aware that you might see images as well as hearing a voice or voices. Or, you'll see images, but hear no voices.

So, the most important criterion about hearings voices is that when it happens to you, don't panic! Be open to it. Remain receptive. Don't judge. Just listen.

3

THE CREATIVE EDGE

"Logic will get you from A to B. Imagination will take you everywhere."
—Albert Einstein

In 1972, Regency Press published a novel, *Black Abductor*, by Harrison James, a pseudonym for James Rusk, Jr. It's about a terrorist group led by a black man who kidnapped a college student, Patricia. Her wealthy father was well-known and had right-wing sympathies.

In the novel, Patricia was kidnapped near campus while she was with her boyfriend, and was badly beaten by the abductors. For a while, he was a suspect in the case. The fictional Patricia initially resisted her captors but eventually subscribed to their ideology and became a champion of their cause. The terrorists sent Polaroid photos to her father and described the abduction as America's "first political kidnapping." They predicted they eventually would be surrounded by police, tear-gassed, and wiped out.

Two years after the book was published, in 1974, Patricia Hearst, daughter of newspaper baron Randolph Hearst and then a college student, was abducted from her apartment near campus. The kidnappers were members of the Symbionese Liberation Army, a terrorist group led by a black man. Her boyfriend, Steven Weed, was with her at the time, was badly beaten, and became a suspect in the case. Patricia Hearst, like the fictional Patricia, became a sympathizer of her abductors' cause. She ended up robbing a bank with her kidnappers and was photographed carrying an MI carbine.

The FBI was either familiar with the novel or had read it and the author became a suspect in the case. The real-life abductors were eventually surrounded by the police, tear-gassed, and killed, just as the fictional kidnappers predicted they would be. So, had the terrorists read the novel? Or was this an instance where a creative edge enabled an author to sense the future so deeply that he uncovered stunning details identical to those that came about two years later?

CREATIVITY & PRECOGNITION

Creativity is like a wolf, howling at the moon. It surges up from somewhere deep within, you throw your head back, and this incredible sound rushes out into the world, transforming everything in its path. It's usually defined by four words that begin with "i": imagination, inventiveness, inspiration, ingenuity. Synchronicity is rarely mentioned. And yet, creativity and synchronicity are like twins conjoined at the hip. They share organs, skin, blood, the life force. They complement and nurture each other. In fact, without meaningful coincidence, our creative endeavors often fall flat. We're able to take an idea just so far and can't make that final leap into something larger than ourselves that speaks to the human collective.

Creativity is the way our consciousness interacts with our physical environment to usher something new into the world. It's a way of being, a lifestyle, a state of mind. It's at work in every facet of our waking, conscious life and hums along while we sleep and dream. It's our companion when we travel, undertake something new, fall in love. It's the force behind everything we do.

Not surprisingly, it enables us to tap into what Carl Jung called the collective unconscious, a kind of primal sea, a psychic repository of our history as a species, a place where past, present and future exist as one. This inner space is what author Stephen King , writing in *The Craft*, calls "dreaming awake," when he merges with whatever he's writing.

We all experience those magical moments of merging—when

we're listening to certain music, watching a stunning sunrise or sunset, playing with our kids or pets, engaged in some activity that we enjoy. These moments can happen anywhere, at any time, under almost any circumstance, even when we're faced with a crisis, need to make difficult choices, or seek confirmation about something important.

Jung, who coined the term synchronicity, considered it an umbrella for all psychic phenomena and abilities. For example, knowing what someone is about to say on a subject unrelated to your conversation could be called telepathy or precognition. But it's also synchronicity—an experience where two similar events come together outside of cause and effect, and the resulting coincidence is meaningful to the observer.

There are numerous instances of writers experiencing synchronicity when they are so plugged into their stories and characters that the rest of the world disappears. But it isn't the exclusive domain of writers. Musicians, inventors, innovators, painters, movie and TV directors, actors, and performance artists all experience it. And so do teachers, nurses, doctors, engineers, politicians, parents, kids.

SCIENCE FICTION VISIONS

Science fiction writers have a long tradition of envisioning the future and its technology that later becomes scientific fact.

Take Jules Verne. In his 1870 novel, *Twenty Thousand Leagues Under the Sea*, he imagined an underwater ship powered by electricity. American inventor Simon Lake was inspired by the novel and invented his own submarine, the *Argonaut*, in 1888. Verne's novel, *From the Earth to the Moon*, published in 1865, described the details of a space capsule that in 1969 sent astronauts to the moon—the *Apollo 11*. He stipulated how long the flight would last, that it would be launched from Florida, and its splashdown in the ocean. He also described light-propelled spacecraft now known as solar sails. And keep in mind that Verne was living in the time of the Civil War.

Verne isn't unique. Throughout history, numerous examples exist of how writers, artists, moviemakers, and others in creative professions depicted inventions and details about future events that they realistically had no way of knowing. But Verne, as a science fiction writer, may hold the top prize in this regard.

Edward Bellamy is probably best known for his 1888 *Looking Backward*, a utopian novel set in Boston in 2000. In the story, the U.S. is a country that exists in a spirit of cooperation and brotherhood—not exactly what life is like in the twenty-first century! However, the people in his utopia carry cards that allow them to make purchases without cash. Sounds a lot like a debit card!

Robert Heinlein's most famous novel was probably *Stranger in a Strange Land*. But like many writers, he started out writing short stories. In 1941, he published *Solution Unsatisfactory* in *Astounding Science Fiction*, about a future world where the U.S. develops an atomic weapon that ends WWII. This event launches a nuclear arms race. The story was written before the U.S. entered WWII and five years before the bombing of Hiroshima and Nagasaki.

In 1953, Ray Bradbury's *Fahrenheit 451* describes "little seashells... thimble radios", portable headphones already existed, but they were massive and heavy. Bradbury's "thimble radio" describes earbuds, which didn't come into wide use until 2000. With the popularity of wireless earbuds, the "little seashells" became an even more apt metaphor.

Then there's the 1969 novel *Stand on Zanzibar* by John Brunner. It takes place in 2010, a man named Obami is president, terrorist attacks and school shootings are rampant, cell phone video chats are a favorite way to communicate, cars are powered by rechargeable electric fuel cells.

William Gibson's 1984 novel *Neuromancer* predicted the World Wide Web, virtual reality, cyberspace, and hacking a decade before the Internet existed as it does today.

In May 1982, Stephen King published *The Running Man* under the pseudonym Richard Bachman. The story is set in the U.S. in 2025. Life is a dystopian nightmare, the economy lies in ruins, and Ben Richards, the protagonist, is desperate. He's unemployed, his daughter is gravely ill, and his wife is now prostituting to help pay the bills. He undergoes rigorous training so he'll be chosen to participate in The Running Man, the most lucrative show of Games Network. He'll be hunted by the network's elite killing team and if he manages to survive thirty days, he'll win $1 billion.

In 1987, the novel became a movie starring Arnold Schwarzenegger. In September 1989, a TV reality show, *American Gladiators*, premiered that had some uncanny parallels to *The Running Man*. Minus the death threat.

These examples are just a small cross section of science fiction novels that presaged the future. Did these writers, through their creative endeavors, dive into the archetypal well of ideas where time doesn't exist? When novelists are plugged into their stories and characters, they envision the inventions, gadgets, society and government they describe.

But what happens when a group of writers get together and work on scripts for television or movies? Well, take a look at *Star Trek*.

One of the most famous *Star Trek* gadgets was the communicator, which looks similar to the cell phones of today. Martin Cooper, who oversaw the invention of the first mobile phone in the '70s, directly credited *Star Trek* for inspiring his vision. Then there's the PADD, a device first seen in *Star Trek: The Next Generation* in the late '80s. The PADD, or Personal Access Display Device, bore a strong resemblance to today's Android and Apple tablets, and had a similar smooth, flat, touchscreen interface.

While several movies and TV shows predicted the touchscreen interface, the film *Minority Report* was most accurate in predicting how universal touch technology would become. In 2013, researchers at the University of Bristol announced "ultrahaptic" technology, which allows for touchscreen technology without the touching—just like in the movie.

The movie *Eternal Sunshine of the Spotless Mind* imagined a procedure where memories can be erased. In 2013, scientists were testing a drug that blocked certain types of memories in animals with a single dose. Three-month-old memories of lab rats were erased, and weeks later, there was no sign of the memory returning.

The 1990 film *Total Recall*, based on a short story by Philip K. Dick, portrayed high-speed, full-body security scanners. In 2016, Boston-based Evolv Technology announced plans for the first public trials of A.I.-powered high-speed body scanners.

One of the most interesting twists in all this is that in January 2017, the month Trump was inaugurated, George Orwell's 1949 novel *1984* made a fresh appearance on the bestseller list; the book predicted several aspects of the modern world. Even though we haven't arrived yet at the post-nuclear dystopian state Orwell wrote about, by the summer of 2019 it became clear we have a president who cannot be charged with a crime, and a Congress whose power to investigate the president was being actively blocked—two major steps toward a dictatorship.

VISIONS & ART

Art, like writing, is a process of immersion. An artist immerses herself in color, shapes, forms, images, seeking to express something internal—an idea, an emotion, a fragment of dialogue, a taste, touch, something sensory and ineffable. When artists, like writers, plug in so deeply to what they're creating that only the easel and brush and paints exist, they can easily tap into future events that can be both personal and global.

In his book *The Sense of Being Stared At: And Other Unexplained Powers of the Human Mind*, British biologist Rupert Sheldrake notes that in his database of 312 cases of precognitions, seventy-six percent of them concern dangers, disasters, or deaths. This coincides with data gathered by the Society for Psychical Research between the 1880s and the 1930s, which found that 174 out of 290 cases—sixty percent—concerned deaths or accidents.

"It is unlikely that selective memory alone can account for this predominance of dangers, deaths and disasters in reported cases of premonition," Sheldrake writes. "There are strong evolutionary reasons for this bias. In people, as in animals, natural selection must have favored the ability to sense impending disasters."

But what about precognitions connected to events more than

a decade in the future? Can artists, like writers, tap into something that far ahead?

ALEX GREY'S ART & GLOBAL PRECOGNITIONS

Even when creativity takes us into the global arena, the message isn't apparent for some time. Many of the paintings of visionary artist Alex Grey fall into that category.

One of his most famous paintings, *Gaia*, was based on a vision he had in 1988, on the day his daughter was born, and it was both "hopeful and terrifying."

The terrifying part of the painting depicts a tremendous tree that rises in the center of the painting, its trunk vivid and alive with people, faces, esoteric deer, birds, a lion, and other wildlife. Pristine mountains loom in the distance, topped by an unpolluted sky, clear and blue.

To the right of the tree, branches burn, gray smoke spews from smokestacks and a nuclear plant containment building and sullies the sky. Power lines slice through the painting on both sides of a highway. The New York skyline rises against the horizon, the Twin Towers clearly visible. A pair of commercial jets are visible in the polluted skies near the towers.

At the base of the tree, on the right, stand two men. One wears black clothing reminiscent of a terrorist and the other bears an eerie resemblance to George W. Bush. At Bush's side, a penis the size of an adult rises from the ground. As Grey explains in a YouTube video, it's "a dick." As in, Dick Cheney. The painting is a disturbing rendition of life before and after 9-11.

Grey's vision in 1988 propelled him straight into the collective soup of the future, where he tapped into a mass event thirteen years before it happened and a dozen years before Bush was elected to the presidency. In that place where such deep creativity occurs, time dissolves.

"...we all possess the ability to see the future," writes Michael Talbot in *The Holographic Universe.*

If that's true, then the question becomes: How much of the future—global and personal—do we really want to see? And can any of it be changed?

This possibility is explored expertly in *Travelers*, a Netflix series that started in October 2016. The premise is simple: Hundreds of years in the future, the last surviving humans have discovered a way of sending consciousness back through time, directly into people in the twenty-first century. These travelers assume the lives of their hosts and work as teams to change certain events in the twenty-first century that will save humanity from the terrible future they have experienced. Armed only with their vast knowledge of history and an archive of social media profiles, they discover that their successes in altering history are making it more difficult for them to accomplish their ultimate goal.

JESSIE, THE GOLDEN RETRIEVER

When art taps into a personal precognition, the results for everyone involved can be delightful! In this instance, it was about a dog.

Years ago, our daughter's third-grade class was given an assignment connected to Thanksgiving. The kids were supposed to create a sculpture from clay that expressed their gratitude for something in their lives. Parents were invited to the class presentation the day before the Thanksgiving holidays began.

The day of the show-and-tell, Megan stood in front of her class and presented her little red clay sculpture. "I'm grateful for the Golden Retriever I'm going to get," she announced. "And this is the dog."

Her sculpture certainly looked like a Golden Retriever right down to the ears, the tail, the body stance, the shape of its head. We looked at each other: *Huh?* We had three cats and no intention of getting a Golden Retriever or any other dog.

A couple of weeks later, a friend of Megan's asked if we would like a dog. The friend's father was a school cop who trained dogs to sniff out drugs in lockers and one of their dogs, a Golden Retriever, had washed out of the program. No dog, nope, nope, we said.

And then we saw her, a beautiful reddish-gold retriever

about three years old, who had been given up by her original family when the son developed asthma. Now she had washed out of the drug-sniffing program, and was going to end up at the pound unless someone adopted her.

"We'll try her for a few days," we said. "See how she and the cats get along."

Well, Jessie came into the house, the three cats came over, sniffing, checking her out, and Jessie's tail wagged and wagged, and then she plopped down in front of Rob's desk and then in Megan's doorway, and that was that. She stayed for eleven wonderful years.

When Trish's mother went into an Alzheimer's unit, Jessie accompanied us each night for a visit with Rob, Trish, Megan, and Trish's dad. Many of the residents knew her by name even though they didn't have a clue who we were. There were three women who were always on their way into Manhattan for dinner and a play. Two of them were dressed to kill, the third wore her pajamas and big Barney the Dinosaur slippers. Jessie would accompany them to the locked front door, where they believed their taxi awaited them, the magical Cinderella coach that would take them into New York.

"Where's the cab, Jess?" Lillian would ask.

Jessie's tail wagged, she barked, and the women waited at the locked door, in the locked ward. For Jessie, all humans were worthy of love and affection.

When Megan and her friends played music and sang for the residents of the unit, Jessie waited patiently, listening, her paws seeming to tap to the music, her tail swishing rhythmically.

We took Jessie everywhere—to the gym, the grocery store, vacations. She captured the hearts of everyone with whom she came into contact. Her love was always unconditional. She taught us about love. Family. Community. Every afternoon, Rob took her down to the park in our neighborhood to play Frisbee. Kids would gather around, get into the Frisbee groove, and pretty soon, we'd have teams. Jessie had her own fan club. Everyone in the neighborhood knew her—and she knew them.

At the end of Megan's freshman year at college, Jessie made the trip across the state with us, but she wasn't feeling well. It was hideously hot that day, mid-90s, no breeze, and she was suffering. One of us remained in the car with her, air conditioning blasting, while Megan's stuff was loaded into the car. On the way back across the state, we stopped to let Jessie out and she could barely stand. That night, one of our cats stood vigil next to her, and we knew the end was near.

We took her to the vet the next morning, early, fast, and discovered she had some sort of throat problem—she couldn't swallow, the prognosis sucked. Surgery that might not work, drugs that would cripple her. We opted for euthanasia. At the moment the vet injected her, her eyes flicked to each of us. She was aware, cognizant, she knew. She had gone the extra mile to wait until Megan was home again before she left. She had arrived when Megan was eight. She departed when Megan was nineteen.

Eleven years. In the grand scheme of things, it's not that long. But her impact on our lives was profound.

That third-grade presentation is a great example of precognition, an aspect of synchronicity. Megan not only knew we were going to get a dog, she got the breed right!

It's one thing to read about other people's experiences of precognition through art or any other means. But it's an entirely different thing when you experience it yourself, within your family, and it concerns a dog who became an integral part of your tribe.

Interestingly, that early sculpture may have been a peek into Megan's own future as an artist who specializes in wildly colorful portraits of animals—many of them dogs, but also cats, turtles, elephants, birds. Just give her a photo and away she goes.

ART & THE I CHING

The *I Ching is* a Chinese divination system that's at least 5,000 years old. It was introduced to a larger Western audience in 1950, through the translation of Richard Wilhelm, a European who spent most of his life translating the ancient Chinese texts. The system is based on sixty-four patterns known as hexagrams, which are derived by tossing three coins six times. You receive either solid or broken lines. When you toss a six or a nine, then the lines change—a broken line six changes to a solid line and a solid line nine changes to a broken line, which yields a second hexagram. In the system, the changing lines suggest that whatever you asked about is in flux and the second hexagram is the outcomes.

In all, there are 384 possible combinations of lines.

Adele Aldridge, an artist and devotee of the I Ching, has undertaken a huge project—illustrating and defining all the 384 combinations. But she has chosen to use seven illustrations per hexagram, one for the image at the beginning and then an illustration for each of the six lines. So that's 448 images! It's a mind-blowing ambition.

In March 2017, she was working on Hexagram 26, *The Taming Power of the Great*, defining and illustrating line two. In the Wilhelm translation of the *I Ching*, this line is defined as *"The axletrees come off the wagon."* Adele's interpretation is that you are *stopped by circumstances.* Her illustration of the line depicts the wheel of a horse-drawn carriage on the ground and a woman leaning back into the carriage, struggling to move it off the road.

At the time, she had been sick with the flu and one particular day, she was too sick to even work. But she needed litter for her cat, so she decided to run to the market and, as she put it, "at least do something."

However, en route to the market, she crashed her "ancient Honda Civic" into a pole in the parking lot and totaled it. While she sat in the parking lot waiting for AAA to come, she became disheartened that the I Ching hadn't warned her about this in her morning reading. "In my misery and shock, I thought, *So much for the I Ching. It doesn't work. Maybe I should dump the I Ching.* A most ridiculous thought but that was the state I was in." So, not only had she totaled her car, but her worldview was in crisis.

"After I was home from the entire misery scenario with my car dragged away for junk, I looked at the I Ching reading I had gotten for the day that morning. It was #49, *Revolution*, changing to #20, *Contemplation*. *Revolution* is what Wilhelm calls #49. But these days I also check Alfred Huang's, *The Complete I Ching* for his input, which is always interesting. I was stunned to see that he calls hexagram 49 *Abolishing the Old*. Now, abolish is a strong word. My car was abolished. But my belief in the I Ching was restored."

Several days later, Adele was able to return to her art work and was stunned to realize the scene she'd been painting at the time she crashed her car was not only a synchronicity, but a precognition. Her illustration of the line with the woman and the broken-down carriage literally illustrated her pending situation. Through her art, she had sensed the future.

Are we, through our creative endeavors, able to dive into the archetypal well of ideas where time does not exist?

THE COMIC BOOK WRITER

Comic book writer Doug Moench experienced one of the most frightening examples of telepathy—or clairvoyance—we've heard of.

In the 1970s, he wrote and worked on Planet of the Apes for Marvel Comics. It was one of Marvel's longest-lived series and featured original Ape stories as well as adaptations of the various movies. In 1975, it ran eleven issues that included color versions of the adaptation of the first two films, which Moench wrote.

On one particular day, Moench had just completed writing a scene for a *Planet of the Apes* comic book about a black-hooded gorilla named Brutus. In the scene, Brutus invaded the hero's home, grabbed the man's partner by the neck, and held a gun to her head so the hero would do what he demanded.

Just as Moench finished writing the scene, he heard his wife calling for him from the other side of the house. He thought her voice sounded strange. He hurried across the house and when he entered the living room, saw a man in a black hood with one arm around his wife's neck and his other hand clutching a gun that he held to her head.

"It was exactly what I had written…it was so immediate in

relation to the writing and such an exact duplicate of what I had written, that it became an instant altered state," Moench told Jeffrey R. Kripal, who wrote about the incident in *Mutants and Mystics: Science Fiction, Superhero Comics, and the Paranormal.*

We initially felt this incident was precognitive, but it occurred so closely to when Moench was writing the scene that it's more likely it was telepathic or clairvoyant. The intruder, after all, had to find a way to enter the house, then get inside and seize Moench's wife. Or, was the intruder already inside the house as he began writing the scene?

After the experience, Moench found it difficult to write. He was afraid that whatever he wrote might happen. "It really does make you wonder," Moench said. "Are you seeing the future? Creating an alternate reality? Should you give up writing forever after something like this happens? I don't know."

Moench didn't give up writing. But Kripal noted that the black-hooded figure became his obsession for months, then years.

We couldn't help wondering if Moench was creating a reality through the act of writing that particular scene. This may not be as farfetched as it sounds.

Quantum physics tells us that subatomic particles exist in a state of potential until they are observed or thought about. If, as physicist David Bohm suggested, consciousness rises from the implicate or enfolded order that exists beneath our daily lives, then we can impact developing events through the intense focus we experience during the creative process, visualization, meditation, and other ways.

Perhaps, like with any other skill, it simply takes practice and determination.

4

FUTURE KNOWING

"What you got, son, I call it shinin' on, the Bible calls it having visions, and there's scientists that call it precognition. I've read up on it, son. I've studied on it. They all mean seeing the future."
—Stephen King, The Shining

A SENSE OF KNOWING

It's known as precognition and presentiment, but these visions of future events are more commonly referred to as premonitions or omens. It's an ability that many of us associate with psychics, card readers, fortune tellers. However, we don't need to look elsewhere for hints about what is to come. Frequently when a premonition comes to us, it involves a particular incident, something troubling, unknown or unsettling. When the answer appears as insight, it's often accompanied by an uncanny sense of knowing, a sentiment that on the surface might seem unlikely and illogical.

In *The Intention Experiment: Using Your Thoughts to Change Your Life and the World*, author and researcher Lynn McTaggart suggests that the future "already exists in some nebulous state we actualize in the present." Former Stargate remote viewer Joe McMoneagle thinks that his future self sends requested information back in time to him. He explains in his book, *Mind Trek:* "In other words, at some point in the future, I will come to know the answer to whatever question has been put to me in its accurate form. That is when I send it back to myself in the past."

We had a cat named Fox who disappeared one day. When a couple of days passed and she was still missing, Trish was certain something had happened to her. She wasn't just lost, but maybe she was injured or killed. Another day or two passed and no one who lived in our building had seen the cat. That's when Rob blurted, "Fox will return by midnight Saturday." He felt an uncanny certainty about it.

Three days later, a couple of minutes before midnight on Saturday, our next-door neighbor knocked at our door, holding a tabby cat in her arms. She told us she'd just spotted Fox in the courtyard outside our door. Her paws were covered with cuts, like she'd been clawing to get out of something. She also smelled of perfume as if a woman had been holding her.

In another instance, Rob lost his billfold in a neighborhood lake while windsurfing. He'd forgotten to take it out of his pocket. Yet, in the aftermath he refused to cancel his credit cards and order a new driver's license. Again, he'd experienced an odd sense of knowing. Illogical as it seemed, he was convinced the billfold would be returned to him. Maybe it wasn't lost in the lake after all, he told Trish, and would turn up somewhere else.

Wishful thinking. The wallet was definitely at the bottom of the lake. We know that because several days after losing it, a man who was fishing with a net scooped it up. He called Rob and the next day Rob went to his house and recovered the wallet with cash and cards intact. Adding to the unlikely convergence of events, Rob had met the man a week earlier when he'd come to our house seeking business for his landscaping company.

What is the source of this feeling, this sense of knowing that an event is going to happen? Dr. Bernard Beitman, a psychiatrist and professor at the University of Virginia, writes in *Connecting with Coincidence*: "There must be mechanisms by which energy-information (E-I) like this can be converted into electrical nerve impulses the brain can process into emotion and behavior."

Beitman includes a story of a man who drove to a place in the woods where he had never been. He didn't know why he was going there, but when he arrived he found his sister about to commit suicide. "How did the brother 'feel' the danger? How did he 'know' how to get there?" He suggests that "a map with a GPS-like route" linked with his brain, but did so outside of the man's awareness.

For most of us, these experiences manifest spontaneously and often in strange, complex ways. For artist and writer Adele Aldridge, a particular image of a man was enough to evoke feelings in her that, years later, reached fruition. Again, it was a sense of knowing that generated the emotional texture that ultimately manifested in a surprising way.

Once a week for several years, Adele drove to her psychologist's office near the Metropolitan Museum and on the West Side Highway, passed a huge billboard of the Winston cigarette man. The image haunted and riveted her and she realized she hated this man. He struck her as narcissistic and filled with contempt for women. Just seeing his image on that billboard enraged her.

Six years later, after she'd moved to California, she met the Winston man—though she didn't recognize him initially—and got romantically involved with him. Lived with him. And all the negative aspects she had sensed about him during those drives when she saw the billboard unfolded in their relationship. She had sensed the future in one of the most peculiar ways we've heard about. But that's how precognition works. It uses whatever is readily available to get its message across.

THE BRAIN AND PRECOGNITION

In Larry Dossey's book *The Power of Premonitions*, he points out that recent research shows that the hippocampus in the brain may be involved in premonitions. It makes sense. The hippocampus is the center of emotion, the autonomic nervous system, and memory.

Researchers at a neuro-imaging center at University College London studied five patients with amnesia who had suffered brain infections that had damaged the hippocampus. They could recall the names of relatives, but not past events. When they and a control group were asked to visualize *future* scenarios, common events like visiting a beach or pub or meeting up with a friend and to describe what it would feel like, they couldn't do it.

"The hippocampus-damaged subjects could not describe spatial relationships between objects that were part of the future scenario, and they said little about what they felt like," Dossey writes. "The discovery that the hippocampus is involved in visualizing the future may be important in understanding premonitions."

This element may be key in understanding the science of precognition because people who experience it visualize possible future events. Dossey points out that a major difference is that the individual experiencing the premonition often experiences a *certainty* that the event will occur. The person who visualizes a future event considers it imaginary. "The brain may not respect this difference. It has a way of responding as if the imagined event is real."

If, for instance, you're lying in the dark, are the only person in the house and hear noises that sound like a door opening, then like footsteps, it's possible that you're imagining it, but your brain doesn't know that. It reacts as though the event is *real* and releases stress hormones that prepare you for the real thing.

Is the hippocampus in people who experience precognition more active and ramped up than the hippocampus in people who never experience it?

Eleanor MacGuire, the same researcher who conducted the experiment with the amnesic patients, performed MRIs on sixteen London cab drivers. She found that the rear region of their hippocampuses were uniformly larger than that of the fifty individuals in the control group.

As Dossey explains, becoming a licensed cabbie in London isn't easy. "Drivers have to learn 'the knowledge,' as it's called, which includes up to twenty-five thousand street names and the locations of all the major tourist attractions. Cabbies must know not only how to get somewhere, but they must know the most direct route possible." This "knowledge" usually takes three years of training. The longer a cabbie is on the job, the larger that region of the hippocampus became.

When the BBC News featured MacGuire's discoveries, some cab drivers came forth and said their experiences as cab drivers made them better at everything from business decisions to mathematics. MacGuire is against GPS devices in London cabs. "We believe this area of the brain increased...because of the huge amount of data they have to memorize. If they all start using GPS, that knowledge base will be less and possibly affect the brain changes we're seeing."

Dossey points out that GPS devices may not be the only inhibitors of precognition when it comes to technology. Practically instantaneous information on everything from the weather to stocks to who will win the Super Bowl may inhibit our natural precognitive ability as well.

SO WHAT'S THE SOLUTION?

Realistically, most of us won't go off the grid. But perhaps if we unplug for brief periods every day and spend a few minutes envisioning and visualizing the future we hope to create, it will help develop whatever precognitive abilities we have.

On the other hand, maybe you don't have to unplug. All of us have access to precognition through any type of altered state.

In January 2016, Trish was trying to recall the last time she'd had a precognitive experience of any kind. There had been a few small things, mostly through impulses or remembered snippets of dreams. Then she remembered that in October 2015, during one of Rob's meditation classes, she had set an intention before the class. She asked to receive information about when her novel would sell. It had just started making the rounds with publishers that month.

Toward the end of the class, when she was in a really relaxed and receptive state, several words popped into her head: *around new moon, November 11*. She knew that new moon would be in Scorpio, her rising sign, and felt hopeful.

In astrology, new moons are always about new beginnings, new opportunities, new doors opening. Opportunities often come out of nowhere. And when one falls in your sun or moon sign or in the sign of your ascendant, the opportunities that manifest themselves are usually really good ones. Two weeks after a new moon, there's a full moon, the time of harvest and completion. We often receive news on or around the time of a full moon.

So on November 11, she kept waiting for the phone to ring or for her agent to email her that the novel had sold. Instead, she received an email from mystery writer Nancy Pickard, suggesting that she write a short story for *Ellery Queen's Mystery Magazine*. So Trish did. She submitted it, then felt annoyed that her apparent precognition about the sale of her novel hadn't panned out.

For the next few days, she remained hopeful since the new moon energy can manifest itself for a few days on either side of the actual date. But by November 14 or so, she started wondering what that impression she'd gotten during meditation was really about. Then, on the evening of December 9, about thirty-six hours before the new moon in Sagittarius, she received an email from the editor at *Ellery Queen* saying she would like to buy the story.

From this, Trish learned that her original impression about a *new moon* sale was correct. It meant a sale, but not necessarily of her novel and not necessarily by or on the next new moon. But the November 11 date was important because that was when Nancy had suggested she write the short story the magazine bought shortly before December's new moon. In other words, Nancy's suggestion was the opportunity, but it was up to Trish to take action.

Back in October when she'd had the impression, she didn't have any intention of writing a short story. And because she specifically had asked for information about when the novel would sell, it never occurred to her that the *new moon* hint might pertain to something else.

And that's the tricky thing with precognition. We don't always have the full details when we sense the future and our left brains immediately intercede and start trying to connect the dots about what it may possibly mean.

PRACTICE: HOW TO BE A PRECOG

In the movie *Minority Report* starring Tom Cruise, three psychics—called precogs—recorded crimes before they happened for "pre-crime" authorities, who then swept in and arrested the future perpetrator in advance of the crime. You may not be as talented as those movie psychics, but there are ways to bolster your precog IQ.

Remain open to the possibility that you can glimpse the future. If you think it's impossible, then you're going to prove that belief to be true—at least for you.

Your awareness plays a big role. People who are interested in mysteries of the unknown have a better chance of being a precog than those who are overly skeptical, fearful, or closed to the possibility.

Remembering and recording your dreams is a great starting point. (More on that below.) You can request a dream about the future.

Watch for signs and symbols that appear, especially startling ones, like a vase falling and crashing just as you were talking or thinking about something coming up in your life.

Try programming a precognitive event. Pose a question about something you want to see in your future. Say it aloud, write it down, or do both. Then pay attention to the first thing you see or hear. Maybe it's the lyrics of a song on the radio, something said on the TV, a telephone call, or maybe it's a pop-up ad on your phone or computer. Whatever it is, try to interpret it related to your question.

SIGNS AND SYMBOLS

Precognition often comes through signs and symbols—a particular song we hear, a book that falls at our feet, an animal that crosses our path, a sequence of numbers or a name that crops up repeatedly, an event or incident that hits us viscerally, and yes, even through billboards. Synchronicity is often a component.

We live in a collective sea of these signs and symbols. Nature, the Universe, Source, God, whatever you want to call it, constantly chatters to us. But we're so mired in the business of physical life that we don't always hear that voice. Or we hear it and ignore it. Or we hear it and think, *Yeah, sure, I'm kinda losing it here.*

You're in your car. Maybe you're on a road trip. Or picking up your son or daughter from school. Or maybe you're about to back out of your garage to head off to the grocery store, the park, a friend's house. Your car dies. You turn the key and nothing happens. On the surface, it's an annoying, inconvenient, and common event. But on another level, the abrupt and unexpected nature of the event could be a sign or symbol of something that's about to happen.

When our daughter was in elementary school, Rob would take her to school and Trish would pick her up. On one particular day, she was in the pick-up line and her car suddenly went dead. There she was, the car refusing to start, cars behind Trish honking at her to move forward.

Rob drove over and jumped the battery and followed Trish and Megan home. Once in the driveway, it was dead again. Clearly, a new battery was in order. But was there something more, an underlying message? When we're in the midst of such events in our daily lives, it's easy to overlook them as possibly symbolic. But sometimes the meaning pops right out at you. Trish was about to call AAA when she noticed a message on our answering machine from a writer friend. Our literary agent of fifteen years, who had jumpstarted our careers, had died suddenly of a heart attack.

Standstill. The battery dies. The car has to be jumpstarted.

If there are no accidents, as Robert Hopcke theorizes in his book by the same name, then the death of the battery coinciding with our hearing about the death of this agent wasn't random. Just how are all of us, the dead and the living, connected, anyway? How are we connected to the larger world beyond us? We think of it as synchronicity, that phenomenon that exists in the space between what we see and what we sense, that border between what quantum physicist David Bohm called the implicate (enfolded) order—the underlying reality—and the explicate (unfolded) order—the physical world and everyday reality. The inner, the outer. The non-local and the local mind.

DREAMING THE FUTURE

When we dream, we slip away from the daily world and connect with the deeper order of reality where past, present and future blend. In dreams, messages from the future can appear as symbols or they can be direct and unmistakable. Sometimes, they can be a blend.

That was the case of a dream told to Rob by a man who had contacted him because Rob knew one of the women intertwined in the mysterious saga of famed writer and anthropologist Carlos Castaneda. Like many of Castaneda's avid fans, John firmly believed Castaneda's stories were simply straight-forward retelling of actual events rather than semi-fabrications. So when he explained his dream to Rob, it wasn't surprising that he rejected Rob's interpretation of the dream as symbolic.

In the dream, John said that his family's cabin was tilted sideways, like the foundation was crumbling, and then it collapsed. Since most dreams shouldn't be taken literally, Rob advised him to look at the symbol of a crumbling foundation. Was there something in John's life that seemed to be falling apart? Unknown to Rob, John and his wife were contemplating a divorce. In spite of the apparent symbolism related to the foundation of his marriage, John remained concerned that there was something wrong with the foundation of the cabin.

A couple of weeks later, John contacted Rob and told him that he had driven four hours to the cabin over the weekend. "And guess what? Two concrete blocks on one corner had slipped. The cabin really is in danger of tilting and even slipping off its foundation. We've got people working on it this week." John added that he and his wife had resolved their differences and were getting along better.

In this case, it seemed that the dream was both symbolic and literal. It symbolized the need for John and his wife to shore up their relationship, if they were to remain together. It also alerted

John to the deteriorating foundation. His conscious mind might not have registered it, so his "dreaming self" brought it to his attention.

One of the best-known precognitive dreams was revealed by Abraham Lincoln, and it has become an unforgettable part of his legacy. In early April of 1865, he told several people that in a dream, he heard strange sounds of mourning in the East Room of the White House. According to Ward Hill Lamon, one of those friends, Lincoln said he came upon his own body lying in state. In his book, *Recollections of Abraham Lincoln: 1847–1865*, Lamon quotes Lincoln from that conversation. "Before me was a catafalque on which rested a corpse wrapped in funeral vestments. Around it were stationed soldiers who were acting as guards, and there was a throng of people, some gazing mournfully upon the corpse." Lincoln couldn't see the face so he asked a guard who it was. "The president," the guard in the dream said.

Three days later, Lincoln was assassinated.

In his autobiography, *Memories, Dreams, Reflections*, Carl Jung relates a dream in which he was attending a garden party. His sister was there with a mutual friend from the town of Basel, a woman whom Jung knew well. In the dream, he knew the woman was going to die. But when he woke up, he couldn't remember who the woman was, even though the dream remained vivid in his mind. "A few weeks later, I received news that a friend of mine had a fatal accident. I knew at once that she was the person I had seen in the dream but had been unable to identify."

Sigmund Freud opened the door to the scientific study of dreams in his book *The Interpretation of Dreams* in 1899. While Freud was mainly concerned with their psychological meaning, it was Jung who explored dreams as a path to psychic awareness, including precognition. Jung believed that, rather than disguising our psychological needs, dreams reveal them. He thought that dreams expose hidden conflicts or problems and offer hints about the future.

PRACTICE: YOUR DREAMS OF THE FUTURE

We all dream, but we don't all remember our dreams and we definitely don't remember *all* of our dreams. Vivid dreams often occur shortly before waking up, and therefore are easier to remember. Most of us spend between 90 and 120 minutes a night in REM sleep, and if we've been involved in high-intensity creative work before we go to bed, that's often where our psychic dreams focus.

Some of us ignore our dreams or consider them an unimportant part of life. Precognitive dreams, though, usually stand out from ordinary ones in their clarity, but also in your reaction. You might wake up feeling energized, startled or surprised. Make an assessment on your own dreaming.

Do you remember your dreams?
I often remember multiple dreams
I occasionally remember dreams, but quickly forget them
I rarely recall them
I don't believe that I dream
How often do you think about your dreams?
Daily
Occasionally
Rarely
Only when I have a nightmare or startling dream
Never
Do your recall any dreams that predicted a future event that occurred?
Yes
No
Maybe. The event hasn't happened yet.
What value do you place in your dreams?
Very important
They provide guidance
They are of little importance
I try to avoid thinking about them

PRACTICE: INTERPRETING YOUR DREAMS

If your intent is to find out if your dreaming self is prepping you for future events or even revealing what is coming, you need to make a concerted effort to remember your dreams and interpret the symbols.

The first step in remembering your dreams is to keep a dream journal or a recording device near your bed. Before you fall asleep, tell yourself several times that you will remember your dreams, especially any dreams related to the future. When you wake up, don't dismiss any dreams as unimportant or nonsensical, don't make any judgment call. Simply write down whatever you remember. Often when you recall one dream, a second dream comes to mind.

After you've captured your dream, take time to interpret its meaning.

See if you can connect the dream events with anything going on in your life. Such dreams are called processing dreams, but they can also provide insight that you might've missed.

Look for any metaphors or puns that might pop out. If you dream of a snake slithering through the grass, beware of someone entering your life who might act deceitful, like a "snake in the grass." Or, say you dream that someone gives you a spoonful of cough syrup. As a metaphor, "taking your medicine" suggests that you must do whatever is necessary to accomplish a goal. Alternately, if you are getting "a taste of your own medicine," you soon may be paying the consequences for something you did. Which one applies?

Follow your feelings. How you feel about a dream might be as important as its contents. Note your feelings about the other characters in your dreams as well as the action. For example, does a stranger in a dream make you feel uncomfortable, angry, frightened, happy, or amorous?

Monitor your dreaming self. Pay attention to yourself in your dreams. After all, you're always there, either as an active character or as an observer. How do you look, how do you act? If you look older, you could be tuning into a dream of the future.

Notice your actions. Could they be revealing something coming up in your life?

Look for a message. Your dreaming self might have a message for you, possibly something related to a future event coming your way. It might come as a symbol, or it could be delivered verbally by a dream character.

FEELING THE FUTURE

That's the title of a study that appeared in the *Journal of Personality and Social Psychology* in 2011 by Daryl Bern, a professor at Cornell University. His experiments involved 1,000 Cornell students viewing erotic photos that incited them to glimpse the future. The students were shown an image of two curtains on a computer monitor and they were directed to select the curtain that hid an erotic photo. The idea was that such stimuli normally produces certain human responses. The question was whether the response could be obtained before the stimulus occurred. In essence, the students were asked to "feel" the future—the curtain hiding a photo of explicit sexual activity.

The answer was a resounding yes. Across all 100 sessions, participants correctly identified the future position of the erotic pictures more frequently than the fifty percent hit rate expected by chance. The results were 53.1, considered statistically significant.

Ben Goertzel, a scientist who reviewed Bern's experiment for *h+ Magazine*, asked why, if precognition exists and we are all precogs to varying degrees, weren't the results of the experiments higher? Then Goertzel answered his own question: "Of course, outside the lab, people have reported many apparent cases of extremely dramatic psi effects. But in the long history of parapsychology lab research, going back far before Bern to [J. B.] Rhine's ESP work in the 1930s, shows that when you bring psi into the lab, it tends to become more of a systematic statistical biasing factor than a source of individual mind-blowing 'miracle' events."

Interestingly, when students were asked to find non-erotic photos, their accuracy dropped to about fifty percent, what would be expected by chance. Laboratory studies of paranormal phenomena have also shown that subjects are less successful when they are not told the ongoing results of their efforts.

INSTANT PRECOGNITION

Many people have premonitions of events that are about to occur within seconds. Here are a few examples:

You intuitively slam on your brakes even though you've got a green light, and a moment later a car traveling on the cross street runs a red light.

You think of something a moment before another person expresses your exact thought, even though you weren't talking about the subject.

You think of an unusual word or phrase, then a moment later hear the exact same thing on the radio or television, or from someone passing by.

PLANETARY EMPATHS

Some people, it seems, have an ability to tune into "mass events"—happenings that affect large numbers of people—before they occur. They don't know what's going to happen, but they know it's going to be "earth-shaking," affecting our collective awareness. We've been researching these individuals, whom we refer to as "planetary empaths" since 2011, have collected their experiences, seeking common threads.

An empath is a person who has an ability to tune into another person's emotions, and sometime literally take on those feelings. "They feel everything, sometimes to an extreme, and are less apt to intellectualize feelings," writes Dr. Judith Orloff in *The Power of Surrender: Let Go and Energize Your Relationships, Success, and Well-Being.* A planetary empath, on the other hand, is someone whose entire physical being reacts to global mass events that are about to unfold.

These individuals are so attuned to the planet that they experience physical, emotional and psychic symptoms hours and sometimes days, or weeks before a natural or man-made disaster.

They come from different countries, different cultures, different ethnic and spiritual backgrounds, and a large majority of the ones we've interviewed are women. Their symptoms are most intense just prior to the disaster, and often quickly subside once the cataclysmic event has occurred. Debra Page, a paranormal researcher and psychic in Pennsylvania, is one of them.

"Even though I was born intuitive and empathic, nothing prepared me for how those qualities would progress through life," Debra wrote in an e-mail. In the early 1990s, she began to notice that her intuitive flashes were expanding to include world events. The curious thing was how these flashes translated into physical symptoms.

Days before a world event, she would feel a profound grief and heartache that nearly crippled her. "Then I started noticing a pattern. The grief episodes would precede an event—either a natural or man-made disaster—and disappear when the event happened. Among them: Princess Diana's death, the beginning of the Gulf War, the shooting at Columbine, at Virginia Tech, the 2008 financial debacle."

Debra and her husband, Larry, were out running errands on December 23, 2004, when she suddenly experienced a loud, sustained ringing in her left ear. Visions of destruction and flooding swept through her. "I knew many would die. I was so disoriented my husband had to hold me up until it was over. I told him what I was witnessing. I was horrified. I knew it would happen in three days, but didn't know *where* it would happen."

Three days later, on December 26, a 9.1-9.3 mega-thrust earthquake jolted Sumatra, Indonesia, setting off a series of deadly tsunamis that inundated coastal communities with waves up to 100 feet. At least 230,000 people were killed in fourteen countries, including India, Sri Lanka and Thailand, making it one of the deadliest natural disasters.

DIVINING THE FUTURE

Divination systems date back into pre-history and today remain popular tools for exploring the future. The tried and true systems—tarot, I Ching, runes, astrology—have spawned numerous books, decks of cards, and games. All of them are tools for peering into the future and are accessible to anyone who invests the time and energy to learn the system's unique language.

We have worked with and written about a number of divination systems, have gotten readings from psychics who use various methods and tools to predict the future, and have studied divination in other cultures. A common thread exists. When you ask your question and the cards are drawn, the runes are thrown, the chart is cast, a moment in time is frozen. The particular probability depicted is the one most likely to happen.

However, if you asked the same question a week from now, it's likely you would receive a different answer because probabilities continually change. But regardless of what's depicted, even a fantastically positive probability doesn't guarantee that the event, relationship, or circumstance will occur. It means that on your current path, the *potential* makes it the *most likely* scenario. Your free will, intentions, passion, and actions are the triggers. A natal chart in astrology works on the same premise.

A natal chart is based on your exact time, place, and date of birth, details you—or your soul, your higher self—chose before you came into this life. It's a blueprint of your *potential*, of what your soul hopes to accomplish and experience this time around. The moment when you drew your first breath became a snapshot in time. How that potential unfolds depends on the choices you make.

When our daughter was born, Trish noted the exact time she was delivered. Three days later, she drove over to a New Age bookstore to have Megan's chart drawn up. This was in the days before PCs were common and astrology apps were a thing of the future. She knew enough about astrology to interpret parts of the chart herself, but didn't want to read something into it that wasn't there. *Virgo sun and moon, a picky perfectionist with an eye for detail. Pisces rising—artistic talent, imagination, empathic, and maybe some victim stuff going on. Sagittarius at the midheaven, so she may travel in her career.* But it was Renie Wiley who really fine-tuned Megan's chart.

She sat at our dining room table, staring at the chart for a few minutes, then started talking. "This Sagittarius midheaven, Trish.

She's going to work with animals, maybe as a vet, but certainly in some capacity. She's artistic, intuitive, and her imagination surpasses yours and Rob's. She'll be a communicator, might even be a writer, like you two. But mutli-talented.

"Uranus, Neptune and Saturn in Capricorn in the tenth house... forget any idea you have of her ever having a normal nine-to-five job. Pluto in the eighth—she'll inherit money. And she'll be on the same page you two are in terms of the psychic realm. And look at this loaded seventh house! This girl is going to have a lot of friends. She's feisty when it comes to work, will be disciplined about her pursuit of health...."

She kept talking specifics for twenty or thirty minutes and Trish jotted notes. Now, thirty years later, the accuracy of what Renie said that day is spooky.

Megan always has had an affinity for animals. Her first word, at seven months, was *cat.* We had numerous types of pets while she was growing up—cats, dogs, a guinea pig, hamster, bird, and always, the animals were her friends. She attended a charter school for acting, starred in a short film she'd written, and became more aware of her artistic leanings.

In college, she majored in art and spent a month of independent study at Dolphins Plus, a dolphin rescue facility in the Florida Keys. When she was a sophomore, she and a friend volunteered at an animal rescue facility in Ecuador, where she worked with monkeys, toucans, and other wildlife endemic to the country.

Her tenure at Dolphins Plus resulted in a series of dolphin paintings for her final college thesis that are extraordinary in the use of color. Her first job out of college was at Disney, working with dolphins. She hated the bureaucracy, the nine-to-five routine, but fell in love with the dolphins. Today, she's an entrepreneur. She spent four years teaching art classes as an artist for Paint Nite, specializes in pet portraits, is a dog walker and dog sitter, and has just completed her first novel.

So, did Renie read Megan's future? Or has Megan simply pursued the potential inherent in her birth chart? Or is it both? It's like that silly conundrum about the chicken and the egg: which comes first? Does it really matter?

Einstein contented that our divisions of past, present, future were artificial constructs, that all time exists simultaneously, *now*. And Jung, in his exploration of the human psyche, stumbled upon his concept of the collective unconscious, a repository of experiences, symbols, and knowledge that is common to all people, that is, in essence, timeless.

So when we talk about future knowing, maybe we're simply tapping into Einstein's flow of time, into Jung's collective unconscious, into a matrix science still doesn't understand. Maybe those of us who sense the future are the explorers, the pioneers, and what we learn will flow into the collective consciousness of humanity.

PRACTICE: STICHOMANCY

Here's a system that's quick and easy, and can be surprisingly accurate. Think of a question or issue that concerns you. Take a few moments to focus on it. Then open a book and randomly stab your finger at a line. See if the word or phrase your finger touches illuminates your question or concern. We find that dictionaries work best for us. Some practitioners favor using a Bible or other religious texts.

The symbology of the source you use should also resonate for you. In other words, if you've never read the Bible, that probably wouldn't be the ideal book to use. On the other hand, if you're a fairy tale buff, try *Grimm's Fairy Tales*. Think of your question, open the book to a random page and with your eyes closed, point at any spot on the page. See if the word, phrase or sentence your finger touches addresses your question. You might also take note of the fairy tale involved.

If you're using a dictionary, look at the word you're pointing at, the surrounding words and especially the word that's being defined. Also, note the word above and the one below. You might find further clarification. However, if a nearby word defined on the page is opposite in meaning, that might indicate the matter you asked about could go either way. In any case, if the meaning is ambiguous, close the book and ask again for clarification. You might also re-phrase the question so it's more specific. However, avoid asking endless questions or superficial ones. You'll tend to receive superficial answers.

Here's an example of a reading from a dictionary. The question is: *What are the benefits of using divination to seek answers to concerns?* Using a dictionary, the word that was randomly chosen was *lift-off.* That could indicate a starting point for finding a resolution to an issue. The word above was *lift* and the first definition was: *raise or remove to a higher position.* That could mean that divination is about raising an issue, or removing it as an issue by taking a higher stance or position on the matter.

Finally, when Rob asked for a clarification, the word he received was *Mecca.* And the definition was: *a place one aspires to visit.* That suggests that divination is one means to attaining what you are seeking, an answer.

IS THE FUTURE FIXED?

One of the questions that arises regarding precognition relates to free will. If it's possible to glimpse future events, does that mean the future is fixed? Is that true for individuals as well as mass events where many people might somehow see the future unfolding before it happens?

On the surface, it seems that if it's possible to see future events, then the future is already set and we have nothing to do but play our prescribed roles. However, when we see potential trouble ahead and take corrective action, the event we glimpsed is either altered or our action allows us to avoid involvement.

The late Dr. Ian Stephenson, a professor of psychiatry at the University of Virginia Medical School, researched psychic experiences related to the sinking of the *Titanic.* He found nineteen documented cases of passengers who had premonitions about the voyage. Some of the nineteen heeded their premonitions and declined to board the ship. Others ignored their premonitions and died. Stephenson detailed the cases in an article published in 1960 in the *Journal of the American Society for Psychical Research.*

Those passengers who cancelled their trips changed their

future, an apparent act of free will. But the others among the nineteen also had free will and consciously or otherwise chose to ignore their hunches. Those who decided not to sail altered their futures, but had no effect on altering the event itself. So the sinking of the *Titanic* could be seen as a mass event—one affecting large numbers of people—that was likely to happen.

The question of whether or not we have free will is of particular interest to psychics who portend to see the future. If they can do so, doesn't that mean it's predestined? That's the question that psychic Erin Pavlina, author of *The Astral Projection Guidebook: Mastering the Art of Astral Travel,* discussed on her website. "For the past several months, I've been trying to understand and determine if we are all living scripted lives that we cannot change or if we have free will and the ability to completely change our fates. It didn't seem to me that both can be right at the same time."

Finally, she asked her guides, who provided an explanation. They told her that before we are born, our higher self confers with more advanced spirits who help plan the next life. Major life events will be established—selecting your parents and any siblings, your career and a life plan. Here's how they explained it: "Imagine there's a maze in front of you and it represents your life. At one opening is your birth and way across the maze is another opening that is your death. Inside the twisting corridors of the maze, our higher self and those other spirits place major life events. Think of it like placing cheese in a maze for a rat to run around in. Those events are placed there on purpose. This is the predestined aspect of your life. How you end up arriving at each of those events is where free will comes into play."

Perhaps mass events, such as the World Trade Center disaster and the sinking of the *Titanic,* are chosen by our collective unconscious as a way of jolting us from our narrow focus on the daily world. That jolt enables us to glimpse a larger picture that recognizes we are all interconnected, that we are all on the same boat in our evolutionary journey. Yet, within such seemingly inevitable events, individuals maintain their free will and can opt out of participating directly.

JANE ROBERTS AND SETH

For years, author and mystic Jane Roberts channeled Seth, "a consciousness no longer in physical reality," as he described himself. Together, they wrote twenty books on the nature of physical reality. In *The Individual and the Nature of Mass Events*, Seth talks about our physical reality as being divided into what he calls Framework 1 and Framework 2. In the first, our normal conscious daily life, free will is fully operative as we make choices to experience certain relationships, circumstances, situations.

But in Framework 2, "...all the details will be arranged, the seemingly chance encounters...the unexplained coincidences that might have to occur before a given physical event takes place."

Seth's Frameworks 1 sounds a lot like David Bohm's explicate order and Framework 2 sounds like his implicate order. Bohm theorized that everything, even space and time, unfolded from the implicate.

"In the creative atmosphere of Framework 2, all intents are known... no act is private...Each mental act is imprinted in the multidimensional screen of Framework 2," according to Seth.

Furthermore, Seth contends: "Your world, then, is the result of a multidimensional creative venture...in which each person and creature, and each particle, plays a living part. In Framework 2 each event is known—from the falling of a leaf to the falling of a star, from the smallest insect's experience on a summer day to the horrendous murder of an individual on a city street."

All these events have a meaning in as larger pattern of activity, Seth says. "That pattern is not divorced from your reality, not thrust upon you, not apart from your experience. It often only seems to be because you so compartmentalize your own experience that you automatically separate yourself from such knowledge."

Perhaps people who sense the future believe it can be done and are simply better able to tap into Seth's Framework 2 and

Bohm's implicate order. They do so in ways suited to them as individuals.

In an audio clip from the Seth audio collection (Volume 1, Tape 2, Selection 1, Excerpt E) Seth said: "You form your experience... You form your past, your present, and your future. You are responsible for each daily moment, individually and en masse. En masse, your beliefs bring about the world conditions that you know. Individually, they form your intimate daily life... Your beliefs become reality. What you believe IS, and becomes real in your experience. There are no other answers. There is no area in your life to which this does not apply."

If Seth is right, then we—the collective consciousness of humanity—create these mass events through our beliefs. And if we create them, then we all have the ability to tune in on them. Some of us tune in through our bodies or through dreams, visions, and other altered states. Mediums and channelers tune in through spirits. And some of us tune in through impulses, hunches, synchronicities.

5

OUT-OF-BODY ADVENTURES

"Always know and remember that you are more than your physical body."
— Robert Monroe

It's one of the most unusual types of phenomena—leaving your body and flying off in a second body. These experiences typically happen spontaneously, are startling, and short-lived. They may occur once or twice, then never again. But some people learn to master the technique for entering OBEs and directing their adventures.

Others are naturals, like Robert Monroe, founder of the Monroe Institute, which explores the nature of consciousness, especially out-of-body experiences (OBEs). Monroe, who wrote *Journeys Out of the Body*, the seminal text on the subject, was concerned that he was going crazy in the 1950s when he started lifting from his body as he lay in bed trying to sleep. Eventually, he heard about yogis who traveled out of body, and decided not to fight it any longer. He was worried that he might die, but he committed himself to going with the experience. After that, he gained more confidence and soon was able to initiate the experience and even explore realms beyond the physical world.

One day in the spring of 2004, our daughter came home from high school and told us that one of her friends was going out of body *all the time.* We asked what she meant by all the time. "Like almost every night when she lies on her back." Megan replied. "She lifts straight up and she can see herself lying on the bed below her."

The teenage girl was frightened and disturbed by the repeated out-of-body experiences and so was her mother, who took her to a neurologist. She was given a CAT scan and to the relief of the girl and her family, there was no sign of a tumor or other brain disorder. She was told that her "imaginary" experiences were probably related to stress, and she was prescribed a drug to block any further OBEs.

The neurologist thought the experience was related to the functioning of the girl's brain, not her spirit. However, science writer Michael Talbot in his book, *Beyond the Quantum*, offered another point of view when he described an out-of-body experience from his teen years. At first, he thought he was dreaming, but everything in his dream seemed real. Nothing was distorted and nothing about his appearance on the bed below him or the furnishings of his room had changed.

"I floated weightlessly out of my bedroom and into the living room, still marveling at the fact that all of the features of the house seemed identical to how I knew them in my waking state.... Suddenly, as I swam like some airborne fish through the rooms, I found myself heading on a collision course with a large picture window. But before I had time to panic, I drifted through it, effortlessly, and looked back in astonishment to see that my passage had not affected it in the least."

He continued drifting along, looking at the dewy grass below him, then suddenly he spotted a book in the grass. He moved closer to it and saw that it was a collection of short stories by the nineteenth-century author Guy de Maupassant. While he was aware of the author, he had no knowledge of the book or any particular interest in it. After that, he lost his awareness and fell into a deep sleep.

The next morning on his way to school, a neighborhood girl joined him and said she'd been walking in the woods near his house and thought she might've lost a library book. She told him it was a collection of short stories by Guy de Maupassant and asked him if he'd seen it. "Stunned, I related to her my experience of the night before, and together we strolled to the spot where I had seen the book in my dream," he wrote. "And there it was, nestled in the grass exactly as it had been when I had lazily floated over it."

Talbot thought his OBE could have been a dream that, in a remarkable coincidence, mirrored a real-life incident—the lost book and its exact location. A second possibility was that information about the lost book had entered his consciousness even though he didn't realize it. Talbot noted numerous studies that show the mind has a remarkable ability to pick up information without our consciousness awareness of it. In other words, Talbot might've seen the missing book in his peripheral vision without realizing it. However, he wrote that he had not walked in the area during the time the book was missing, nor had he talked to his neighbor between the times when she lost the book and they recovered it.

The other explanation was that a part of his consciousness left his body during his sleep and he actually had seen the book. Talbot added that the explanation was the most likely of the three, based on the impact of his own experience as well as cases that he'd read about.

Monroe was convinced that out-of-body travel is more common than we think, that we go out of body often in our sleep, but don't remember. That said, a true OBE is one in which we consciously recognize our personal identity while we are separated from our bodies. Rather than dream-like images, an out-of-body traveler might float near the ceiling in a second body and see his or her own room and body just as it is, sleeping on the bed. Frequently, people who experience their first OBE become either frightened or excited and fall back into their physical bodies within seconds. Unlike a dream that might dissipate from our memory within minutes, out-of-body travelers tend to remember the experience, and recall the sensation of being awake and out of body. They also might remember details of places they've never visited and later verify the existence of the location.

The joy of realizing that it's possible to travel out of body and even initiate and direct one's adventures is a game-changer. It's a realization that the world is truly magical, and seemingly impossible things can and do happen.

WHAT SCIENCE SAYS

Meanwhile, in spite of countless descriptions of seemingly wondrous out-of-body experiences, mainstream science finds nothing magical about OBEs. The consensus is that these experiences are hallucinations created by misfiring neurons. Neurologist Jason Braithwaite and colleagues, in a 2011 study, linked OBEs to "neural instabilities in the brain's temporal lobes and to errors in the body's sense of itself." Braithwaite reported that the "current and dominant view is that the OBE occurs due to a temporary disruption in multi-sensory integration processes."

In 2003, Terence Hines, a professor of neurology, wrote that spontaneous out-of-body experiences can be generated by artificial stimulation of the brain and this strongly suggests that the OBE experience is caused from "temporary, minor brain malfunctions, not by the person's spirit (or whatever) actually leaving the body."

Neuroscientist Dean Mobbs, at the University of Cambridge's Medical Research Council Cognition and Brain Sciences Unit, says there's nothing paranormal about near-death experiences when a flatlining patient travels out of body. Mobbs and co-author Caroline Watt, in a study published in the October 2011 issue of *Trends in Cognitive Sciences*, contend that such experiences can be biologically explained.

In spite of such research, these types of studies don't explain cases in which someone who is out of body accurately sees or hears things that the person's physical body couldn't possibly have noticed. Some of the most documented cases come from near-death experiences in which revived patients recall conversations in the operating room or describe medical procedures that they couldn't hear or see.

TRACKING A NEAR-DEATH EXPERIENCE

One of the best documented stories comes from medical social worker Kimberly Clark Sharp, who is the founder of the Seattle

International Association for near-death studies. In 1977, when she was a young social worker at Harborview Medical Center in Seattle, her life was forever changed by the experience of a middle-aged Mexican migrant worker named Maria. She described Maria's out-of-body experience in depth in an essay published in *Surviving Death: A Journalist Investigates Evidence for an Afterlife*, by Leslie Kean.

While visiting friends in Seattle, Maria suffered a massive coronary and was rushed to the Harborview emergency room. Several days into her hospital stay she had a coronary arrest. While medical personal attempted to revive her, the heart monitor showed that she had flatlined—she was clinically dead. Fortunately, her heart was shocked into beating again and she was revived, though still unconscious. She woke up several hours later, breathing on her own. However, she was extremely agitated and a nurse paged Kimberly for assistance.

Kimberly had met Maria and was aware of her recent in-hospital coronary arrest. In fact, she had looked in on the team as they had attempted to revive their patient. Maria didn't speak much English and Kimberly's Spanish was basic. But they were able to communicate through Spanglish and gestures.

Maria, it turned out, was excited and anxious to tell anyone who would listen that she had left her body and watched the recovery effort from a corner of the room near the ceiling. She accurately described the people in the room, where they had stood, what they had said, and what they had done. She also correctly described the electrocardiogram machine and how it had produced a long scroll of paper that was kicked under the bed.

Maria then said she had hovered above the doors of the emergency room, and accurately described the view of the curving driveway and the direction that vehicles were parked. She had no view of the entrance from her room. What makes her story truly compelling and ultimately documented is what she next told Kimberly.

Maria said that while out of body she drifted to another part of the hospital and saw a single, large-sized sneaker outside of a window ledge on an upper floor. She moved closer to it and described it as dark blue and scuffed on the side near the small toe area. She said a white shoelace was tucked under the heel.

She asked Kimberly to go find it in order to prove that while her body was dead, she was not only conscious, but was able to float inside and outside the hospital walls. Kimberly thought it would be a fruitless search, but agreed to take a look.

She walked around the hospital on the sidewalk that encircled it, but was too close to the building to see ledges on the upper floors. She couldn't move away from the building because of heavy traffic and a nearby cliff on one side.

She went back inside and decided to look around on the third floor. "I went into the patient rooms, walked to the window and looked down." She found nothing on the ledges on the east and north sides of the building. While searching on the west side, she was stunned when she peered out a window and saw a man's dark blue sneaker. The end of a lace was tucked under the heel, just as Maria had described. After she retrieved the shoe, she saw that the area of the shoe near the little toe that had faced outward was scuffed.

She wrote: "I was shocked. Time stopped. For that first moment I could not support my own body weight and slumped against the glass, hitting it with my forehead. This was impossible."

Kimberly knew that Maria could not have unhooked her IVs and monitor leads, wandered to the other side of the hospital and looked out a window of another patient's room. She would've attracted immediate attention upon leaving her bed. Another far-fetched explanation that avoided out-of-body travel was that someone planted the shoe on the ledge, then convinced Maria to conspire in a hoax.

In fact, Maria had no visitors the day of her resuscitation. Kimberly could not imagine a busy doctor or nurse taking part in such a charade. Besides, why would Maria agree to participate? Beyond that, none of the staff on duty, beside Kimberly, spoke enough Spanish to convince Maria of something so bizarre.

That left Kimberly with one other option: "While unconscious with her eyes closed, with no heartbeat or respiratory activities and a roomful of medical professionals working frantically to resuscitate her, Maria somehow had visual and auditory awareness of distant locations. While I watched her body being thumped and jolted, she was somewhere else."

Strange as it was, Kimberly realized it was the most likely scenario, and that some people experiencing temporary deaths could remain conscious as they traveled out of their body.

Let's look briefly at OBEs from historical records.

ANCIENT TRAVELERS

The ability to separate from the physical body and travel was first described in ancient Chinese and Indian texts. In classical antiquity, Pliny the Elder (ca 23–79 AD) in his *Historia Naturalis* wrote about Hermotinus of Clazomenae, "whose soul was in the habit of leaving his body, and wandering into distant countries, whence it brought back numerous accounts of various things, which could not have been obtained by any one but a person who was present. The body, in the meantime, was left apparently lifeless …. At last, however, his enemies, the Cantharidae … burned the body, so that the soul, on its return, was deprived of its sheath, as it were."

In the first part of the nineteenth century, out-of-body travel was linked to mesmerism, a theory that everyone had magnetic fluids flowing through channels of the body and blockages in these channels was responsible for diseases. Supposedly, the magnetic influence could loosen the link between the body and the soul, allowing the soul to travel and return to the body. One subject named Bruno Binet, while mesmerized, claimed he was able to leave his body. He said: "In the state I am now … I am out of my body, I perceive it seated on the chair; I walk about in my room without being seen or felt by you whom I touch."

A French clairvoyant named Alexis Didier believed that God allowed the soul to travel anywhere. He wrote: "I can transport from a pole to another with the speed of lightning; I can talk with the Cafres [people of Madagascar], walk in China, descend on the mines of Australia, enter the harems of a sultan in less than an hour, without fatigue …."

Spontaneous OBEs

If you've only had one OBE in your life, it probably happened spontaneously while you were starting to fall asleep or just before you came fully awake in the morning. Spontaneous OBEs also can occur during stressful times, when you're ill. People who are critically ill might undergo a near-death experience and find themselves floating outside their bodies as surgeons attempt to save their lives, as in the case of Maria.

A study from 1984 entitled, *With the Eyes of the Mind: An Empirical Analysis of Out-of-Body States*, published by Praeger Scientific, found that people went out of body when they were physically relaxed (79%), mentally calmed (79%), dreaming (36%), meditating (27%), and emotional stressed (23%). Other circumstances included childbirth (4%), having an orgasm (3%), drinking alcohol (2%), and driving a vehicle (2%). Other spontaneous OBEs have been reported during non-life-threatening accidents, anesthesia, hypnosis, while suffocating, after being shot, even while dancing or talking, according to a report in *Medical News Today* in their July 19, 2017 issue.

The newsletter included an incident reported by a thirty-six-year-old police officer during her first night at work. "When I and three other officers stopped the vehicle and started getting [to] the suspect [...] I was afraid. I promptly went out of my body and up into the air maybe twenty feet above the scene. I remained there, extremely calm, while I watched the entire procedure—including watching myself do exactly what I had been trained to do."

AWAKE, ACTIVE, AND OUT OF BODY

While most OBEs happen when you are in a relaxed state lying down or sitting, researcher Carlos S. Alvarado, a psychologist and a research fellow at the Parapsychology Foundation, has studied cases of people who experience spontaneous separation from their bodies while they are awake and physically active. In 2000, he published a paper, *Varieties of Anomalous Experiences* for the American Psychological Association that reported a long-distance runner's out-of-body experience.

The thirty-two-year-old Scottish woman was training

for a marathon when the event occurred. She described her experience this way: "After running approximately 12–13 miles … I started to feel as if I wasn't looking through my eyes but from somewhere else … I felt as if something was leaving my body, and although I was still running along looking at the scenery, I was looking at myself running as well. My 'soul' or whatever, was floating somewhere above my body high enough up to see the tops of the trees and the small hills."

Alvarado notes that such cases typically occur when the person is performing a repetitive or automatic movement. They also tend to be brief experiences. He mentions a similar case on the website, *Parapsychology: News, History*, involving a sixty-three-year-old English housewife who separated from her body while out walking. "Suddenly I felt a buzzing in my head, then a sudden forceful rush of wind, which came from my entire body. I heard what seemed to be something unwinding. Then I found myself above the wire over the hedge looking down. At first I wondered who that person was below me, I quickly realized I was actually looking down at myself!"

Unlike the perspective of neurologists mentioned above, Alvarado is not so certain about the biological explanation. "We need to be aware that we still do not understand the OBE. It is not clear how the OBE is actually produced and even less what factors determine the specific features of the experience …"

CHILDREN WHO TRAVEL OUT OF BODY

At the beginning of this chapter, we mentioned the case of our daughter's high-school friend who traveled out of body. Researchers report that children as young as six have reported OBEs.

Wesley Meeks, a security chief at a Texas hospital, remembers his first OBE at age ten when he was floating near the ceiling of the bedroom he shared with his two brothers. He watched his older brother get up, turn on the light and go to the bathroom. Then, from just below the ceiling, he saw his brother shake a body in Wesley's bed—his own—and tell him to go to the bathroom. Wesley was instantly pulled down into his body.

When he told his family what happened, he found out that talking about such an experience wasn't appreciated. His mother told him he was just dreaming. His brothers laughed at him, and his father told him to stop making up stories.

The experiences continued, but Wesley Meeks kept quiet about them. He would become a police officer, then a private detective, and today remains involved in a security-related profession. While he has experienced his share of frightening encounters, he ultimately found some benefit in the experiences. He learned how to initiate the experiences and became an adept explorer of out-of-body realms. His journeys have taken him from mundane locations, such as a nearby hospital where his wife was working, to travels into the cosmos.

THE AKASHIC RECORD

One of Meeks' most fascinating experiences involved a journey into the cosmos to a place of knowledge—an enormous mansion—that he later learned was called the Akashic Record. In theosophy and anthroposophy, the Akashic Record is a compendium of all human events and knowledge, both personal and planetary, historical and futuristic. These records are said to be encoded in a non-physical plane of existence known as the etheric plane.

Meeks didn't gain a great deal of knowledge during his visit, but he experienced much more than he had been expecting. We first published a shorter version of this story on our blog, synchroscrets.com and it proved to be a controversial, as we'll explain.

But first the story.

The experience took place during the winter of 2005–2006. Wesley had gone to bed and before getting sleepy, told himself that he intended to have an out-of-body experience. He said he wanted to go to a place he had heard about, the place where knowledge and the events of our lives are stored. At the time, he did not know what the place was called, but he'd read books about OBEs, and some writers told of a huge mansion where all souls live when they are between lives.

"As I began to get a little drowsy, I relaxed from head to toe and began a countdown from nine hundred toward zero. I relaxed, controlled my breathing, and thought about the target of my astral travel. As was usual for me, a ringing started in my head, and soon the vibrations were running head to toe. I felt my body getting heavy. I then mentally pushed and I was out of my body."

Meeks emphasized that he had not drifted into sleep, but was fully conscious when he pushed out of his body. "Next I shot through the ceiling of my residence and up into the night sky. For the first few minutes, the experience of free flight was so exhilarating that I temporarily lost sight of my mission."

He compared the experience to the beginning scene of *Star Trek* episodes in which the *Enterprise* suddenly slams into warp speed and hundreds of stars flash by every second. "It is such a sensation of freedom that I suspect it is the same sensation that people feel when they leave the body permanently. After a few minutes, I absorbed this freedom and exhilaration and was able to focus on my pre-determined mission. I thought that I wanted to see the great mansion. It is mentioned in the Bible when Jesus says, *In my Father's house are many rooms.*"

As soon as he thought about the mansion he was no longer flying at warp speed, but was floating gently toward a massive mansion. He drifted above it and just watched in awe. "There is no way I can even begin to describe the beauty of this mansion, the ornateness, the intricateness of the design and details. It was huge and I cannot even guess at the size. As I floated there, I saw that there were other people floating, some entering smaller compartments in the huge mansion, some leaving the mansion. Some of the people were visible as people, but others were auras of different colors."

AURAS INSTEAD OF BODIES

He somehow knew these auras were the souls of people who had chosen not to appear or to cloak themselves in human bodies. The size of each compartment was about the same as that of a large hotel room, large enough to hold a bed and several pieces of furniture. However, he could see no furniture in any of the rooms. Instead, each room only contained a large vase, two or three times the size of a human body.

"Each vase or urn I saw looked different, and each one was very beautiful, again beyond any description. Some appeared to be of marble, some of granite, some of jade, and other of materials I could not name. There were designs and inscriptions on each vase. The mansion itself was so pure white that it was brilliant, but the floors of each of the compartments were of a material like marble, and so smooth they shone like glass."

Meeks noticed that each compartment had three walls with the fourth side opening into a courtyard. He saw people walking around on the broad sidewalk and sitting in very ornately designed benches. A swimming pool occupied the center of the courtyard and a gentle waterfall flowed constantly into the pool from a ten-foot-high fountain.

AN UNEXPECTED ENCOUNTER

"While I was viewing all this in a state of utter amazement, an older woman approached me. (I was in my forties so I thought she was probably in her sixties.) She was very regal and attractive and was wearing a flowing gown. She asked me if I knew what I was looking at, and I said I wasn't sure. The woman told me to come sit with her on a bench.

"We floated downward and landed on the sidewalk, then walked a short distance to a beautiful bench. We sat down and the woman explained to me that the mansion was built by the Creator and it was so large that I couldn't see all of it at once. She explained that each soul had a room in the mansion, and pointed toward one of the rooms."

She told Wesley that the large vase in the room contained all the knowledge that the soul had gained while going through various lives on the earth and in other places as well. She didn't explain the "other places" and he was too overwhelmed to ask her about them. The woman told him that people lived many lives and spent time between lives by staying on different planes that aren't visible to humans on the physical realm.

DISGUISES

"Then the woman dropped a bombshell. She said that people in the astral realms sometimes disguised themselves for various reasons while they traveled. I did not understand this at all. But she explained that some people didn't want to be recognized or needed to appear different for other reasons, and sometimes didn't use bodies at all, but moved around as auras."

She also told him that people could appear older or younger than they really were on the physical plane or could even be of a different race than in the physical plane. "Then she told me that she was not actually an older woman, but was really my age. She said that she travelled as an older woman both to appear wiser and trustworthy to new travelers and so that some people wouldn't recognize her. I didn't think to ask the whys of all this."

Next, the woman stood up from the bench and instantly was a fairly attractive white female of about forty to forty-five years old. "She wasn't a knockout by any means, but was attractive. Her clothing suddenly vanished and she was nude. At this point I could also see that she had a green aura. I knew telepathically that she wanted to have a sexual encounter with me. Then she said aloud that she wanted to make love, if I wanted to."

AN EROTIC TURN

Wesley realized he was nude as well, and wasn't sure that he had even thought about clothing while he traveled. "So for all I know, I may travel nude all the time. But I was suddenly overcome with both an erotic feeling and the realization that I desired to *bond* with her. I can't explain that term or even how I knew it, I just did. But I remember thinking that all these other people were around and were watching.

"She told me to look around, and I noticed that many people were engaged in what appeared to be sexual contact all over the courtyard as well while floating above it! I realized now that both of us were floating and that I also had an aura that I think was blue."

The woman moved toward him and he embraced her. "I can't adequately describe what happened next, but I will try. While floating we were in a reclining position, the missionary position. I penetrated her, but then somehow part of my very soul or molecules were inside her soul or molecules or both. Our auras merged and we merged, too. *Merge* is the best word I can think of, because we were two, but were literally *one* at the same time."

While they made love in the usual physical way, he felt completely joined in soul and mind. "I cannot even begin to describe the total pleasure, the total ecstasy! Ecstasy is even inadequate. There were vibrations shooting through us that I can sort of relate to as being shocked by a faulty cord or an appliance with a short in it. But it was not painful. It was the greatest pleasurable feeling I have ever had in my life, bar nothing. As pleasurable as sex is, as making love is, this experience was completely off the scale. And the love was total even though we were strangers, but not love like a husband and wife, love like we were all part of one creation."

He didn't know how long the encounter lasted, but he thought the experience lasted longer than most of his other travels combined. "There was a huge climax of energy, not like an orgasm, but more like huge electric shock, maybe like being struck by lightning that lasted for several minutes instead of just a split second. Then we separated."

She told him that he probably needed to go back into his body because the experience was so intense and it was the first time for him. He felt totally exhausted. The woman instantly assumed the form of the older woman again. She told him there was so much for him to learn and that she hoped she would see him again sometime; then she disappeared.

THE AFTERMATH

"I suddenly felt sucked back into my body and was instantly lying in bed awake. I was tingling and vibrating all over. I literally could not move, and I was tired, but exhilarated at the same time." The tingling was so severe that the bed was shaking and he actually thought he would wake up his wife. But the sensation eventually subsided to a dull tingle, one that lasted for three days after the experience.

"For obvious reasons, I didn't tell my wife about this particular incident although I had told her about several of my OBEs. But I could not see what was to be gained from telling her this story. So I typed it and put it in a file on my computer, labeled 'astral adventure'. Then I forgot about that file."

One day, his wife was using his computer and saw the file. She was curious and read it. "She was mad for days, and actually contemplated leaving me, as she looked at the experience as an extramarital affair. So I would certainly counsel my fellow travelers not to mention any such encounters and to protect any related written material with a password or something to prevent what happened to my wife and me. She was hurt badly and was heartbroken. But she eventually forgave and we are doing well now."

Meeks' experience at the mansion was the only encounter of that nature that he ever had. "I've never attempted it again, because for one thing I'm not sure what is to be gained, and also I'm still confused as to whether or not this is actually cheating on a marriage. I have read some who call this cheating and some who say it is not, and that it is beneficial. I do believe that some sort of understanding was passed to me during this encounter. The understanding was that there is an unseen realm and that we apparently live many lives in many forms. But the why of it all was not communicated to me."

REACTIONS

We posted an abbreviated version of the above story on our synchronicity blog (blog.synchrosecrets.com) in 2015. We received several responses from people who say they also have explored astral realms. The reaction ranged from concern that Meeks must have encountered a lower astral being to a more open-minded perspective.

"Hmm...I don't feel good about that," wrote Victoria. "I am aware that people can present themselves however they want to on the astral plane, and have seen it myself, but there must have been some commonality in the energy field to have attracted such a being. In my experience (and I could be wrong) it is usually lower astral beings that still try to merge with humans." She went on to say: "It's my understanding that sexual organs are redundant on the other side. Souls are androgynous until they choose what sex they will be in human form." She added that demons and lower souls can use sex for control.

Natalie, an Australian medium, agreed. "As we evolve through the different planes or mansions, we lose our 'physical shape' more and more and become more subtle in energy. I understand the spiritual merging that Wes was speaking of, but I question the physical penetration bit, and the fact that the being approached him that way. Like attracts like on the Other Side, so he must have been emitting some sort of sexual frequency (maybe subconsciously) or the being was from a lower, more 'physically inclined' plane."

However, Connie, also a medium and a retired hospice nurse, had a different point of view. "There's so very much we don't know as absolute certainties about the multiple dimensions of being. It's likely there are hundreds of thousands of dimensions and we aren't privy to All That Is. I tend to think it may be the better part of wisdom to remain open-minded and ponder the possibility that perhaps dimensions exist in which souls—highly evolved souls—may perhaps have the capability to express in corporeal bodies."

Wesley Meeks, for his part, responded: "I'm not an expert and certainly not a wise being. But I just know that I have only encountered what I believe are human souls traveling on the astral plain, not demons or lower astral beings."

PAST LIFE TRAVEL

After nearly a year, we reconnected with Meeks and asked for an update on his astral travels. In response, the former Texas police officer sent us one of his journal entries in which he described how he had embarked on an astral journey to a monastery where he discovered "himself".

Meeks has both spontaneous and intentional OBEs and this one was intentional, even though he had no idea where it would take him. He found himself in either Mexico or Texas in the 1600s, and he was a Catholic brother. "At this point in my life I had just ended my law enforcement career and was actually in between jobs, so I was 'Mr. Mom.' I woke up around six AM and got my son off to school. Then on this particular morning, I went back to bed in a spare bedroom because my wife, who worked nights, had just gotten to sleep and I didn't want to disturb her."

He laid down and began his ritual to have an out-of-body experience. After only a few minutes of relaxing and forming his intention to leave his body, he felt the familiar vibration and rushing sound in his head. "At first, I just flew, but then found myself kneeling in a small room. It was sparsely furnished, just a small bed, a table and a single wooden chair. I was looking out a small, high window and could see only a square of pure blue sky. At one point, I saw the person, but then I was instantly 'in' the person, and in a split second I realized that I was a monk in a monastery or church compound somewhere in the Southwest."

He somehow knew he was either in Mexico or what would become Texas close to what is now the southern border of Texas. He also knew that he was happy in his situation and at that very moment was praying with gratitude for his position in life. "I don't know how long in 'real time' this experience lasted, but I think it was probably ten minutes or so. I felt in that experience that I was a native of Spain and voluntarily came to this place and was content."

MANIPULATING MATTER

Is it possible to move things while out of body? It's a controversial subject, somewhat similar to the question of whether or not it's possible to move objects with your mind, known as psychokinesis or telekinesis, a psychic ability proclaimed by some. In fact, a substantial amount of experimental evidence has been gathered by parapsychologists in support of psychokinesis. But what about moving objects while out of body?

In one of Trish's rare out-of-body experiences years ago

when she was in college, she was in the kitchen with friends and music was playing on the old-fashioned record player. The needle got stuck and she suddenly found herself in front of the stereo in the living room. When she tried to move the needle, her hand went through the stereo. She realized she was in her second body and immediately zipped back to her physical self at the kitchen table.

While out-of-body travelers move through walls, closed doors, and roof undeterred, can they have any effect on physical matter? Nancy McMoneagle, director of the Monroe Institute in Virginia, told us in an e-mail that her stepfather, legendary out-of-body traveler Robert Monroe, once pinched his wife's arm while he was out of body, and a slight bruise appeared at the spot the next day. But McMoneagle believes that such an ability is extremely rare.

Now comes Wesley Meeks with a story of manipulation of matter that, if true, goes considerably beyond Monroe's pinch. In his correspondences with us, Meeks recounts an OBE to a nightclub where he did something that he's ashamed of and initially didn't want the story published. Supposedly, while soaking up the atmosphere in the nightclub, Meeks reached out as a waitress passed by and hooked a finger over the elastic band on the top of her shorts and pulled them down to her knees. The waitress spun around to find the drunk who assaulted her, but no one was nearby.

When Rob told this story to Nancy McMoneagle, she doubted that someone out of body could do what Meeks claims.

The question of such psychokinetic feats while out of body was a subject that fascinated the late Waldo Vieira, a Brazilian physician, dentist and founder of the Institute of Projectiology. In his book, *Projections of the Consciousness: A Diary of Out-of-Body Experiences*, he refers to the out-of-body condition as the *psychosoma*. He maintains that "the projector should attempt these actions when he feels the psychosoma to be in a denser state. This will facilitate contact with the object and project physical effects." He noted that if the psychosoma were completely empty and immaterial, it would not be possible to act on denser matter.

In his diary entry dated November 1, 1979, Viera describes such an attempt to manipulate matter this way: "I became aware that I was projected as I left the apartment with the target idea of finding a place with switches in order to try switching lights off and on."

He goes on to say, "As soon as I had the idea, a resounding clarification echoed close by, as if it were inside my head. It addressed the fact that when we think, we create. I heard: 'There is a difference between physical objects and the creations of your mind. This bag of toys, for example, is a mental creation.'"

Vieira writes that a bag appeared and seemed to be full of toys. He was told he could pick it up and throw it and the sound it made when it hit the floor would also be created in his mind. He did so and when it hit the cement floor, it made a "tap sound." The voice then assured him that the physical objects he saw were real and that he was seeing them from outside of his physical body.

At that point, Vieira decided to move elsewhere and an instant later saw a wide door near a dimly lit street. He went through the door and found himself on another street, next to a large warehouse similar to those in the dock area of Rio de Janeiro. "Now gliding and totally lucid, I discovered a few light switches in the dark warehouse. As I neared them, I again hear the explanation:

"'You think that you switched the light on. It seems to you as though you have, but you really haven't. Try to observe: what you think of happens, because the will desired it to be so. But the will is only able to affect the extraphysical dimension that you are in right now and not the intraphysical dimension that you are seeing and are appearing to touch, but are really not affecting.'"

Vieira goes on to say that everything the voice predicted came true. When he attempted to move the switches, he firmly felt the movement of the switches on the wall. "It seemed that I had touched and switched them all into the on position; however, the lights did not turn on. The action had merely been simulated."

Finally, the voice said: "Do not concern yourself with

moving physical objects. In order to do that, you would need to expend a lot more of your energies, while your extraphysical body is in a much denser state."

Vieira's story certainly questions the nature of experiences where matter is manipulated from the out-of-body state. However, considering the advice he was receiving, his story opens another question. Whose voice was that?

OBES AND SPIRIT CONTACT

Do spirits communicate with out-of-body travelers? From the diaries and books of many who have mastered the talent, it seems to be the case. Albert Taylor, author of *Soul Traveler: A Guide to Out-of-Body Experiences and the Wonders Beyond*, was frightened by the initial contact from the other side. In an April, 1993 diary entry, he writes that he was floating near his bed when a "humanoid" figure appeared next to him. "Startled, I mentally told it to move away. It did not respond, though it became increasingly transparent. I panicked! I began moaning, hoping that my wife would wake me up, which she did."

That fall, another visitor confronted him moments after he left his body. The incident began when he heard a female voice call out his name. Again, he panicked. "Something or someone was gently holding my arm. Though the grip was more protective than restraining, I initiated the abort sequence, moaning to be woken up." He reconnected and sat up.

"Not only had I seen, felt, and heard an apparition, it decided to communicate. I guessed that if it hadn't been aware of my fear of spirits before, it was now! How patient my guides were during my earlier explorations."

Vieira expresses no fear of the spirits, which he calls *extraphysical* consciousnesses, he communicated with during his OBEs. He even knows some of them by name. In a diary entry dated July 24, 1979, he describes an out-of-body journey one evening through an urban area. He mentions he stopped at a bar where, among the clientele, he counted three people who were out of body and two visiting spirits. He offers no explanation about what they were doing there, but we can assume they were watching the physical beings imbibing spirits! He continued on. "At the end of the Main Street in a small square with a few trees and benches, I came across an extraphysical consciousness who looked like a doctor. His name came to my mind: Calmene. Strong, athletic-looking, blondish and appearing to be about forty-five years old, he was attending to some extraphysical consciousnesses needing assistance.... Upon exchanging mental messages with him, he quickly explained to me that his routine work was helping the needy. At night, the specialized task becomes intense as extraphysical consciousnesses, especially sick ones, enter into contact with persons who are sleeping."

But apparently not all "frequent fliers" encounter spirit guides. Wesley Meeks finds such stories of spirit contact fascinating. But he notes that while he has encountered other out-of-body travelers, he has never been approached by any entities from the other side.

GETTING OUT

Researchers suggest that we might have only one or two out-of-body experiences in our entire lives. However, you can practice methods that others have successfully used to achieve OBEs. There are numerous books available on out-of-body experiences that provide a variety of methods for launching your adventures. Several are listed in the Resource section at the end of the book. They provide a variety of methods. Here are some general guidelines to follow.

Maybe you've had a spontaneous, short-lived OBE and you'd like to get out again. The first step is to move past a casual interest, and create a true desire. For example, the yearning to visit a love interest who is living or visiting at a distant location could create such a strong desire. In fact, there are stories in which that desire is so strong that individuals have succeeded in projecting their apparition to the location and it was seen by one or more people. D. Scott Rogo in *Leaving the Body: A Complete Guide to Astral Projection* discusses such stories, including one of his own. In his case, it was an interest in seeing what was going on in his own house while he was away for an extended stay. The person staying at Rogo's house was so shocked when he heard strange sounds and glimpsed the apparition that he fled the house.

While entering an OBE solely through concentration isn't a method that's often recommended, Rogo points out: "A constant desire to have OBEs, maintained in the mind at all times, seems one way to produce this level of unconscious readiness." At that point, he notes, an OBE might happen spontaneously.

What keeps many of us from moving beyond the casual interest is the fear factor. *What if I can't get back?* Those who have succeeded in attaining controlled OBEs are usually quick to say that getting back into your body is a snap, much easier than getting out. You turn your thoughts to returning to your body, and there you are.

Before you proceed, a couple of cautionary notes are in order. Once you get out, you may find yourself spontaneously entering OBEs, even on nights when you want to sleep soundly. In other words, going OBE could become a chronic condition. That's what happened to Robert Monroe in his early explorations.

Another word of caution relates to how others will accept your experiences. Like Wesley Meeks, you might quickly learn not to talk about going out of body. Friends and family members might think you're making up stories. People close to you might start to act as if they don't trust you. They might wonder what's wrong with you and recommend that you see a therapist. The solution is to find a friend or a group of people who share your new ability. That way you can talk about your experiences with people who are not judgmental and understand what you are experiencing.

Once you've considered those issues and remain intent on journeying out of body, you're then ready to move ahead. A key factor in all the methods is moving into a relaxed state and creating vibrations that run up and down your body. Getting relaxed both physically and mentally is easiest at bedtime or when you're waking up. However, if you have difficulty relaxing or you want to practice getting out of body at other times—such as in the middle of the afternoon—here's a relaxation method you can use to begin your practice.

PROGRESSIVE MUSCLE RELAXATION

Settle down in a place where you won't be disturbed. Lie down, but avoid turning to the position in which you usually sleep. Your intent is to move into a deeply relaxed state for ten or fifteen minutes while remaining awake. With practice, you can reach a relaxed state in a few minutes.

First, take a few deep diaphragmatic breaths, rounding your belly with the inhalation, then letting the belly sink toward the spine on the exhalation. After at least three such breaths, shift to three-part yogic breathing. You start the same way by rounding your belly on the inhalation, then roll the bubble of air upward to the middle of your chest, sniff in a little more air, and roll the bubble to your upper chest. Exhale, releasing all the air and relaxing. Repeat two or three times. Finally, shift to gentle breathing.

You're probably already starting to feel more relaxed, but we're just getting started. Ironically, one way to relax your body is by creating tension in the muscles, joints, ligaments and tendons. By tensing and relaxing body parts, you recognize the relaxed state through the contrast.

Begin with your feet. Curl your toes, tensing your feet, your calves, your thighs and the muscles in your buttocks. Now lift your heels a few inches. Hold for several seconds, then relax. Make tight fists with your hands, tense your shoulders and lift your arms a few inches. Hold for several seconds, then relax.

Next, squeeze your shoulders up toward your ears, hold and release. Now arch your back, pushing your shoulder blades closer together, sliding your tailbone under you. Hold several seconds, then release. Lift your hips, hold, then let yourself down.

Lift your arms and legs, make fists, curl your toes, take a deep breath, hold it and squeeze all the muscles in your face toward your nose. Exhale, then release, noticing the difference between your tensed and relaxed muscles. Finally, roll into a ball with your thighs against your belly, arms wrapped around your shins, forehead toward you knees. Hold and release onto your back with your legs apart and palms turned up.

Take a couple more deep, diaphragmatic breaths. Then slow your breathing. Next, turn your focus from your breathing to your body. Starting with the crown of your head, imagine invisible fingers massaging your scalp. Take your time. Enjoy the imaginary massage.

Now allow those invisible fingers to move onto your forehead and spread outward around your temples. The relaxing sensation moves around your eye sockets, over the bridge of your nose, along your cheekbones, and then down your jaw. Leave a gap between your teeth and let your tongue come down from the roof of your mouth. Relax all of your facial muscles.

The soothing energy flows over your neck, then your shoulders, your upper arms, your elbows and forearms. Let your wrists, hands and fingers relax. Let the palms of your hands relax.

Now the relaxation ripples over your chest and down your upper back, lower back, around your rib cage, and over your abdomen. Your hip bones relax in their sockets and your buttocks relax. The soothing sensation eases down over your thighs. Your kneecaps float on your knees. The backs of your knees relax. Your shins and calves relax. Your ankles, feet and toes relax. The bottoms of your feet relax.

As you continue gentle breathing, relax your circulatory system. Become aware of the beat of your heart and the flow of your blood through the arteries, capillaries, and back through the veins to the heart. Amazingly, the circulatory system extends more than 600,000 miles, twice the distance around the earth. Relax all of your internal organs and glands. Relax... relax...relax.

Relax your nervous system. You have forty-five miles of nerves running through your body. There are about 100 billion neurons (nerve cells) in the human brain, more than stars in the Milky Way. Your brain alone contains a universe unto itself!

Finally, relax your mind. Pay attention to your breathing. Stay in the present moment. Notice how relaxed you feel. Now you're ready to generate the vibrations.

PREPARING FOR LIFT OFF

For some people, the initiation of the vibrations rolling up and down your body is closely related to sleep paralysis, a sense that you can't move or speak for up to a couple of minutes. You might also hear a high-pitched tone or a roaring inside your head. From there, the methods of getting out vary—rising out through the top of your head, sitting up and out, rolling out, or climbing out on a rope, to name of few.

Here's a method adapted from one of the ways that Robert Monroe recommended in his book, *Journeys Out of Body.*

PROTECTION

Since fear is one of primary hindrances to out-of-body travel it's a good idea to invoke protection before launching an out-of-body journey. Monroe suggests using a prayer of protection, such as this one:

I deeply desire the help and cooperation, the assistance, and understanding of those individuals whose wisdom, development and experience are equal or greater than my own. I request their guidance and protection from any influence or any source that might provide me with less than my stated desires.

Invoking protection not only provides an actual safeguard, but it can help you quickly move ahead on your journey by allowing you to eliminate your fears. It also becomes part of your ritual for entering an OBE. As such, the prayer serves as a trigger. In other words, it signals your body that you're about to embark on another journey. You're safe and ready to go.

RELAXING

Move into a relaxed state. You could follow the technique described above. Your goal is to reach that drowsy state between wakefulness and sleep and to maintain it without falling asleep. Set your intention, but don't analyze. Focus and relax. As you become more relaxed and start to drift off, hold your mental attention on something—an idea, an object, even an emotion—with your eyes closed. Once you can hold that borderland state indefinitely without falling asleep, you've passed the first stage.

The next stage is to maintain the borderland state without concentrating on anything. Just focus on the blackness in front of you. Release any anxiety. The third stage involves releasing any rigid hold on the borderland state and drifting deeper into your conscious mind.

CREATING THE VIBRATIONS

The vibrational field that is essential to entering an OBE seems easiest to create if your head is positioned in the direction of magnetic north, according to Monroe. Make sure your room isn't completely dark so that you have some light for a point of reference. Maintain your conscious awareness, but relax as deeply as you can. Then give yourself the suggestion that you'll recall everything you experience that is beneficial to your physical and mental well-being. Repeat the suggestion a few times to reinforce it.

To set up the vibrational waves, imagine two lines extending from the sides of your head and converging about a foot in front of your eyes. Think of these lines as charged wires that are joined, or as poles of a magnet that are connected. Once they converge, extend them three feet from your forehead, and then six feet. Now you must move the intersected lines ninety degrees until they are directly over your head. Then reach out toward the point of intersection through the top of your head.

Keep reaching until you feel a reaction. It may feel like a surging, hissing, rhythmically pulsating wave that roars into your head; let it sweep through your entire body. At this point, your body may become rigid and immobile.

CONTROLLING THE VIBRATIONS

Once the vibrations start, you need to eliminate the fear and panic you might experience. The first time you encounter the vibrations, you might feel like you're being electrocuted, even though there is no pain. To end the session, simply lie quietly and analyze what's taking place until the vibrations fade away on their own.

When you're familiar with the sensation and have moved beyond fear, you're ready to control the vibrations. Mentally direct them into a ring that sweeps around your body, moving from head to toe and back again. Once you've got the momentum going, let it proceed on its own. The faster the vibrations, the easier it is to disassociate yourself from the physical.

It takes practice to smooth out the vibrations. But eventually, you should be able to start the vibrations simply on a mental command, thus eliminating some of the earlier steps.

Focus on a single thought, such as *float upward* or *up and out*. At this point, your thought should instantly translate into action. However, the fear factor might be triggered again. That will bring you back to a familiar place—your body.

SEPARATING AND LIFTING OUT

On your first attempt, you might just separate your hand and explore the area immediately around you. Find an object, maybe something on a bed stand. See if you can identify it by touch.

Once you're out, you can explore your immediate area. If you want to go farther, simply think about where you want to go. The clearer your request, the faster you move ahead to your target. If you want to travel to another city, focus on a particular building or site, such as a park. Alternately, focus on someone who lives there, preferably a person you know.

Your early experiences might be short-lived because of an initial concern about getting back to your body. Once you get past that issue, you might find that you can stay out of body for an hour or more, and even journey into the cosmos. Good luck!

6

PSYCHIC DETECTIVES

"Each person is at each moment capable of remembering all that has ever happened to him and of perceiving everything that is happening everywhere in the universe."
— Aldous Huxley

Yes, they exist—and not just in fiction.

Back in the mid-1980s, we were gathering material for a magazine article on psychic detectives and met artist and psychic Renie Wiley, who worked with police departments on a number of missing persons cases.

In early August of 1981, Renie and a cop from the Cooper City, Florida, Police Department were driving near a mall in Hollywood, Florida, where six-year-old Adam Walsh had been missing for days. The cop hoped that Renie might be able to pick up something psychically about the missing boy—where he was, what had happened to him. At that point, the police believed he'd been abducted, but didn't have any leads.

Renie usually worked with an object that belonged to the missing person, like a child's stuffed toy. She picked up impressions that way. But her only connection with Adam was through the posters of him wearing his baseball uniform and cap. His huge, innocent eyes whispered, *I am your son, your brother, your cousin, your neighbor.* His face had been burned into the collective consciousness and that seemed to be all that Renie needed.

When she and the cop were within a few miles of the mall,

Renie's hands suddenly flew to her throat. She started choking, gasping for air. The cop had worked with her often enough to realize she was picking up something related to Adam and quickly swerved to the side of the road.

"What is it, Renie?"

She sobbed. "Adam was decapitated."

Not long afterward, the head of the six-year-old boy was discovered in a canal in Vero Beach, Florida, more than a hundred miles north of the Hollywood mall.

A PSYCHIC WHAT?

What exactly is a psychic detective? According to skeptics, it's anyone who brings information to police—usually about a homicide or a missing person—that supposedly was obtained by paranormal means.

A more specific definition of a psychic detective is someone with psychic abilities, who has worked with police, and is requested by authorities to look into a case that is puzzling investigators. Typically, psychic detectives are called into a case only after all other avenues of investigation have failed. It's much more common for psychics to approach police with their visions about a murder or a missing person. They may have psychic abilities to varying degrees—as many of us do—but they might also be contacting police for the first time and have no track record regarding success or failure.

In some cases, psychics spontaneously tune into a crime before it happens or at the time of the incident. That's what happened to Jane Clifford, a psychic healer who lives in Wales.

She was lying in bed one night and felt a "blanket of darkness descending over the landscape." She sensed that someone would be murdered in her community and people would be shocked. Three days later, again while lying in bed, she felt blows to her skull with a metal object. A few seconds later, she sensed she was being given a choice to instantly get involved, or not. She decided if she could help in some way, she would do it.

"Then suddenly I'm in this woman's body in her kitchen

and she's being hit from behind by someone she knows and trusted, and I felt her shock. She was unconscious by the first blow, and dead by the third one. I assisted her soul to exit fast and clean. Then I was back in my bed shocked and upset."

She contacted the police after hearing about the murder, confirming her experience. She told them that the woman was struck three times to the right of the crown of her head with a metal object. She said she couldn't see the face of the perpetrator because she was in the woman and looking the other way. The police told her there was no way that she could've known about the three blows, because it wasn't public information.

In Jane's case, she psychically experienced the murder, but couldn't help police solve the case. It turned out that the killer was a neighbor, who the victim trusted, a man who helped her with her garden.

Seven years later, again while lying in bed, Jane experienced the same dark mass moving over the landscape. This time she received specific information: a woman living in the area would be decapitated. Three days later, she flinched and was shocked as she sensed the woman's throat being cut. "Then I aligned with my higher self, feeling the emotions of both without judgment of the perpetrator, and felt compassion for both of them."

The next day she learned that a school boy had decapitated his stepmother. She didn't go to the police in this instance. There was no need for it.

HOW DO THEY DO IT?

Most psychic detectives are clairvoyant, meaning they see events occurring at a distant location, either in the recent past or present. Some, like Renie Wiley, combine clairvoyance (a.k.a. remote viewing) with empathic psychometry, the ability to gain information from an object that the target of the investigation had possessed. Psychometry is considered one of the most challenging psychic abilities to attain and it requires empathic awareness that goes well beyond our normal sense of empathy.

HOW GOOD ARE THEY?

It's hard to come by statistics about the accuracy of psychic detectives. One poll of the largest police departments in the country found that one-third of them had used psychics on some cases. If they were unaware of any sound results by psychics, it's doubtful that many would admit to using them from time to time. Police departments that use psychics do so typically behind the scenes and don't publicize the extent of help received from this non-traditional method of investigation. The stories of success usually come from the psychics themselves or from observers.

It's not surprising that skeptics say that psychics might occasionally make a lucky hit on the whereabouts of a missing person or the identity of a murderer or related details. Their argument is: what about all the times these psychic detectives are unable to assist an investigation or even lead investigators astray?

Over the past decade, their attacks have become more vociferous, perhaps spurred by the popularity of TV series and movies that feature psychic detectives, mediums, clairvoyants. If you Google *psychic detective*, one article after another cites studies where psychics were wrong on cases. Some of the online reviews by skeptics are snide or hostile. One offers this headline: *Psychic Detectives have a Perfect Record*. The record is that they are always wrong, according to the website. Cases are cited in which psychics have said a missing person is dead, only to see the person turn up alive.

The article avoids explaining success stories by simply rejecting them. "On closer inspection, other than anecdotal accounts, there are no documented discoveries of missing persons by psychics." That, of course, is the only way to avoid looking at the overwhelming evidence of psychic successes as well as the decades of scientific evidence attesting to the reality of psychic abilities.

But hardcore skepticism like this misses an important point. If psychics were never successful, police departments and individuals wouldn't bother with them. The problem is *not* that no one has psychic abilities, but rather that people with limited psychic abilities take advantage of the fact that some psychics are successful. As a result, some individuals who have invested financially in such psychics come away disappointed.

In our decades of researching the paranormal, we've noticed that, unlike skeptics, psychics see both sides of the story. From their own experiences, they know psychic abilities exist, but they're also well aware of psychic frauds. They're especially skeptical about psychics who are great at gaining publicity, but have minimal abilities and rely too much on their analytical minds.

Inside Edition decided to test psychic detectives, selecting ten people randomly who called themselves psychics and were willing to be filmed. The interviewer showed each one a photo of a young girl who was said to be missing. All ten said the girl had been murdered. But the photo was actually one of the interviewer herself when she was a young girl.

Clearly, the television show didn't check out the track record of the psychics they chose. Skeptics like the Amazing Randi often target individuals who have already been accused of fraud. Such exposes may provide a valuable service by warning the public to avoid these fakes, but hardly prove that all psychics are frauds incapable of assisting police or anyone else.

In a sense, this selective filtering of information and facts to make a point runs eerily parallel to the current tone of American politics. If you repeat a lie often enough, people start believing it.

Dean Radin, author and psychic researcher, points out in *Supernormal: Science, Yoga, and the Evidence for Extraordinary Psychic Abilities* that scientific reasons exist for accepting that some cases of psychic detective work are valid. "Given that we know from scientific experiments that clairvoyant abilities do exist, the assumption that psychic detectives and psychic spies are always guessing is wrong."

In fact, police in the U.K. in 2015 were told that they

should take information provided by psychics seriously. The recommendation was made by the College of Policing, a professional body for the police in England and Wales.

Under revised professional standards, police were told: "High-profile missing person investigations nearly always attract the interest of psychics and others, such as witches and clairvoyants, stating that they possess extrasensory perception. Any information received from psychics should be evaluated in the context of the case."

NOREEN RENIER

Early in her career, psychic detective Noreen Renier lectured at the FBI academy in Quantico, Virginia, and since then has gained published acclaim from law enforcement authorities. "She helped to locate a plane that contained the body of a relative of an FBI agent," wrote Robert Ressler, a retired FBI agent, in his book, *Whoever Fights Monsters: My Twenty Years Tracking Serial Killers for the FBI.*

The *New York Post* quoted Ressler in an article on June 4, 1988: "The Bureau has used Renier strictly in an academic setting, to expand the thinking of police officers. We have, however, given her name to law enforcement people who want to try a psychic. And some of them have said she's solved cases."

Olin Slaughter, former chief of police for the Williston, Florida, Police Department was quoted in an article the *Williston Pioneer* on June 27, 1996: "Without Noreen Renier we would not have located Norman Lewis. I'm extremely impressed with her abilities. She told us things that she would have to have been an eyewitness to have known."

We met Noreen years ago when she lived in a town outside of Gainesville, Florida. She not only told us about her work as a psychic detective, but also that she was under repeated attacks from local and national skeptic groups, who called her a fraud and claimed she had no psychic abilities. Not surprising, since ardent skeptics don't believe psychic abilities exist. In response, Noreen took one skeptical adversary to court for libel and won.

In 1986, she was awarded a $25,000 judgment against John

Merrell, which he unsuccessfully contested in two courts. A final settlement of $23,800 was paid to Renier in 1992. That judgment included a stipulation that neither party could talk publicly about the case. However, Renier included a chapter, "Psychic vs. Skeptic," in her book, *A Mind for Murder: The Real-Life Files of a Psychic Investigator*, about the case, and Merrell sued her. This time the court ruled in his favor and she was ordered to pay out more than $39,000.

JOE MCMONEAGLE

Some psychics are successful at finding missing people. Joe McMoneagle, mentioned earlier, was a U.S. Army chief warrant officer who became a member of the U.S. government's Stargate program after he exhibited considerable psychic talents. He remained with the project for its entire seventeen years and his handle as Remote Viewer #001 speaks for itself. After the program ended and became public, McMoneagle began offering his skills as a remote viewer in the civilian world. Essentially, he was a psychic for hire, one of the best known and respected in the world.

On May 10, 2003, a film crew from Japan showed up at McMoneagle's door and asked him to help find a missing man in Japan for a television show on psychic detectives. They promised to bring him to Japan to appear on the show if he was successful. McMoneagle agreed, and asked that the name and birthdate of the person be put in an envelope and sealed. At his request, a series of randomly selected numbers was written on the outside of the envelope. That was the protocol of the Stargate project, and the method McMoneagle used. The less information the better. That way his analytical mind wouldn't interfere with his intuitive awareness.

As the crew filmed him, McMoneagle placed the envelope in front of himself while seated at his desk. He cleared his mind, and moved into a meditative state. Gradually, the internal chatter faded away, and *pure* information came to him in the form of images and words. In essence, he was able to project a part of his mind to the location of the missing person.

The first clue he offered was of a large Ferris wheel with changing colored lights all over it. He said he felt it was in Tokyo near water and that from the top of the Ferris wheel you could see four ballfields separated by walkways that formed a cross. One of the walkways ended at a group of sculptures.

Near this complex of ball fields, he saw a river, and across this river was what McMoneagle called a "special railroad track." On the other side of the track was a raised highway that would lead to a multistory hospital, which he sketched as the camera crew recorded his effort. Once they found the hospital, they were to give the name of the missing person to the first nurse they encountered. McMoneagle went on describe the missing person as a man about seventy-seven years old.

When the crew returned to Japan, they started following the psychic detective's clues. They quickly found out that there were thirteen Ferris wheels in Tokyo, but only four of them were covered with lights that changed colors. That immediately narrowed the search to four locations. However, surprisingly, you could see ballparks with intersecting walkways at every one of those Ferris wheels. In all, sixteen ballfields were visible from atop those four Ferris wheels.

Next, the crew began looking for sculptures at the end of walkways, but they couldn't find any. They were ready to give up when they found a topiary garden—sculpted shrubbery—at the end of a path at the last location. That path also ended near the river that McMoneagle had sketched. Across the river, they found a train track. It was a monorail considered very special in Japan, just as McMoneagle had described it.

They also found an elevated highway near the track, and after following it for twenty-eight miles, they came to a hospital. As they left their vehicle, they encountered a nurse walking across the parking lot and asked her if she knew the man they were looking for. To the shock of the crew, she said yes. She knew him, because just a few weeks ago he had been a patient. Did she know where he lived? Again, she surprised the crew. He lived just three blocks from the hospital, and she pointed out the house.

They went to the door and an elderly woman answered.

They asked for the man by name, and she said she would get him. Everything checked out. They had found him! A short time later, the man—missing for thirty-four years and now seventy-eight years old, was reunited with his son, who had instigated the search.

Thanks to McMoneagle's psychic abilities and the tenacious television crew that pursued his leads, the case was solved. In all, by 2004, McMoneagle had made ten trips to Japan and had found seven missing people. Before one of the shows was aired in Japan, Rob emailed his cousin, Russell Walstedt, a nuclear physicist who lived in Tokyo, and asked him to watch the program. Since Russell was skeptical about psychic abilities, Rob was eager to hear Russell's assessment.

After watching the psychic detective program, Russell wrote back. "The remote viewing guy is indeed amazing, if actually genuine." He went on to say that the crew was still looking for two of the three people they asked Joe to locate. However, Russell was baffled by how McMoneagle had located even one of them.

McMoneagle's successes contradict the claims of skeptics that no psychic detective has ever solved a missing person or murder case. The bias against psychic abilities in mainstream science and academia is reflected on Wikipedia, where all forms of psychic abilities and the paranormal are typically dismissed. Psychic detectives, in particular, receive a decidedly negative review with case after case presented in which psychics were wrong. Not a single case of success by remote viewers, such as McMoneagle's, are included. Earlier versions of articles that touted some psychic successes have been edited.

McMoneagle is particularly annoyed by the way Wikipedia summarizes the Army's Stargate program as an unsuccessful venture in remote viewing tasks requested by the army and CIA. The article points out that the CIA dismissed the effectiveness of the project, and suggested that project managers changed the results to make them look better.

We asked McMoneagle for his response.

"They [the CIA] say it didn't work, but returned to our unit more than one hundred and seventy times for more collected data they couldn't do without. If I started a restaurant and invited twenty guests to the opening night, and seventeen of them returned for another meal every night for the rest of the week, would you say the food sucked? Hardly."

He also strongly rejected the contention that project managers changed the reports. He called that assertion outrageous. "To make that statement really shows their ignorance, as well as their fear of RV."

McMoneagle noted that the four volumes of a scientific study, *The Star Gate Archives*, by former project director Edwin May and Somali Bhatt Marwaha, reveal the real story, case by case, of the government's remote viewing program.

BOSTON STRANGLER

When psychics provide accurate information in murder cases, skepticism about paranormal abilities can turn a psychic detective into a suspect. That's what happened to George Hardy, a reluctant psychic detective, who felt it was his duty to tell authorities about his visions.

We met Hardy in the mid-1980s when we were starting out as freelance writers. While seeking sources and information for a magazine article on psychic detectives, we were told we should talk to George Hardy, who had been involved in the investigation of the Boston Strangler case.

Thirteen women were strangled in the series of murders in Boston between 1962 and 1964. We read about the case before meeting Hardy, but found no references to him. Instead, Dutch psychic Peter Hurkos was mentioned in articles that noted he didn't see Albert DeSalvo, the primary suspect, as the killer. DeSalvo confessed to the murders from prison, but later recanted his confession. With no physical evidence linking him to the murders, he was never charged. He died in prison after being stabbed in his cell.

DNA evidence in 2013 linked DeSalvo to the last victim, but authorities have long suspected that more than one killer was involved. Authorities believed that at least eleven of these murders were committed by the same individual because of the similar manner in which each murder was committed.

Hardy was living in Davie, Florida, a suburb of Fort Lauderdale, when we visited him one evening. He told us a disturbing story about his involvement with the case. When he came up with an accurate description about the crime scenes, including details that hadn't been released to the public, he became a suspect. Detectives knew the killer had somehow talked his way into the houses of the women, who lived alone, possibly posing as a repairman. He raped and strangled them with their own nylon stockings. Evidence suggested that none of the victims attempted to flee or fight off the killer.

Detectives wondered if the serial murderer might be working his way into the investigation of his own case by posing as a psychic. They found Hardy to be a serious but amiable man who might be capable of such a feat. When he had told them all that he had seen in his visions, he said the police turned on him.

He was interrogated at length, then injected with "truth serum." Sodium Pentothal is the best-known drug used, but other psychoactive drugs have also been tested and Hardy thought he might've subjected to a drug cocktail of hypnotics and sedatives. In the aftermath, he suffered from a nervous disorder that continued for years. When we talked him in the mid-1980s, he was still afflicted and clearly upset about how the Boston police had treated him.

When we asked Hardy how he'd gotten involved in working with the police, he said that the faces of killers haunt his thoughts whenever he hears about a crime. If he's watching television or listening to the radio and a story comes on about a missing person or an unsolved murder case, he suddenly knows things he shouldn't know, and sees how things happened.

In the aftermath of a South Florida murder case in 1971, Hardy showed up at a police station and said he had information about the murder of George and Ino Jo Beck aboard their fifty-seven-foot catamaran that was docked in Dania, Florida. Hardy described for Dania police the interior of the ship perfectly and gave a reasonable account of the crime. The murder weapon, he said, was a hammer, wrapped in a curtain ripped from a window on the boat and buried behind the killer's house.

Hardy said the killer was a man living near Griffin Road, who drove a bright yellow car and also owned a blue van. He limped on his left leg. The surprised police chief said he knew the man Hardy was talking about. He worked for the local government. After the man found out the psychic had pinpointed him as the murder, the suspect committed suicide a few days later. But the police never found the weapon, in spite of digging up the man's back yard.

Even though he played a small role in the Boston Strangler investigation, the case changed his life. George Hardy died Sept. 21, 2005 at the age of seventy-eight.

It's not surprising that authorities might become suspicious about someone who provides accurate information only known to investigators. But experienced psychic detectives have contacts with police who can vouch for them. In fact, authorities might request help from a talented psychic or even recommend the person to another agency. That was the case with Renie Wiley when she became involved in the investigation of a missing child in a small south Florida town.

THE CHRISTY LUNA CASE

On the afternoon of May 27, 1984, eight-year-old Christy Luna walked to Belk's General Store about 400 feet from her home in Green Acres, Florida, to buy cat food. She never returned. The police suspected foul play, but over the ensuing months, they failed to find any evidence leading to a killer. With no new leads, they asked Renie Wiley for any insight she could provide.

Renie, as mentioned at the beginning of the chapter, had worked with cops numerous times over the years, and agreed to meet with investigators at the Green Acres Police Department. She asked them to bring any toys or stuffed animals that Christy had played with and several articles of Christy's clothing. As a psychometrist and empath, Renie tuned in psychically to energy fields by handling objects that had belonged to the individual or to clothing the person had worn. She also requested the presence of Christy's mother so she could confirm any information that she picked up. Renie knew we were interested in observing her when she worked with cops and invited us to join her.

On a rainy night in the fall of 1984, we accompanied Renie to the police department in Green Acres, a suburb of West Palm Beach with 40,000 residents. Back in 1984, the population was considerably smaller, and as we drove through pounding rain we felt as if we were heading into some desolate outpost at the edge of the Everglades.

Once inside the station, the rain beating down on the roof and windows created an almost hypnotic environment. We were introduced to Christy's mother, then Renie went over to the area where a couple of Christy's stuffed toys and several articles of her clothing had been placed. She slipped off her shoes and twisted her bare feet several times against the floor, grounding herself. Then her breathing deepened and slowed as she entered an altered state. She sat down on the floor and picked up a little bear.

It was a battered bear, worn, well loved. Renie held it to her chest, shut her eyes and rocked back and forth, humming to herself. Even though Renie was a tall, large-boned woman, her body at that moment seemed small and childlike.

She started whimpering, then crying and sobbing, and her body hunched over the teddy bear, as though she were struggling to avoid blows, to protect herself. "The mother's boyfriend used to beat up on her," Renie said softly. "She's deaf in one ear because of it."

The deafness and other details about the girl's health were confirmed by Christy's mother.

With Christy's mother in the room, it's likely that Renie held back some of what she'd felt when she'd clutched the teddy bear. But as soon as the three of us were in our car, with a cop following us to wherever Renie would lead us, she said, "The mother's boyfriend killed her, then took her body somewhere and buried it. I hope I can get a handle on where he buried her."

"Why did he kill her?" Rob asked.

"She came between him and Christy's mother. She was in the way. He has rage issues."

"*In the way?*" Trish blurted. "That's a reason to kill a kid?"

Renie, seated in the front seat, glanced back at Trish. "Hey, he's a nutcase, okay? A sociopath, a sick man."

The rain that sounded so hypnotic inside the station now blew horizontally across the road as Rob drove through the wet darkness, following Renie's directions. *Turn here, turn there, just ahead.* We passed the house where Christy had lived and the store where she had bought cat food and then disappeared. We arrived at a wooded area surrounded by a high barbed wire fence. The cop pulled up alongside of us. Renie felt that Christy's body was buried somewhere in the woods and that the mother's boyfriend definitely had killed her. But her body wasn't found, and without a body, no one was charged.

The entire episode was a fascinating example of how a psychic detective works, but we had no idea that twenty-four years later—seven years after Renie died—the unsolved case would manifest again in our lives.

In the early spring of 2009, several friends were headed into Wellington, Florida, where we were living, for a visit. Among them were Carol Bowman, a past-life therapist and author, and July Scully, a TV writer. Then came a call from another friend, Nancy McMoneagle, now president of the Monroe Institute, who said she would be in our area that same weekend with Dennie Gooding, a psychic from Los Angeles.

We had met Dennie a couple of years earlier through a Canadian astrologer who had recommended her as a psychic. Rob had a reading with her, and we were eager to meet her in person. She said she had been hired by a Palm Beach County sheriff's detective to look into a possible homicide case. The detective knew Nancy, who had recommended Dennie for the job. So, we planned a party.

When you get a group of people together who are intrigued by the paranormal, who see linear time as an illusion, who are open to spirit contact, then it's not surprising that synchronicities flourish.

The day before the gathering, we were going through some old books, weeding out what we no longer needed. A check fell out of one of them. It was dated 1986, made out to us for $50 as a repayment on a loan and was signed by Renie Wiley. We exclaimed about how strange it was that the check had been inside the book all these years, and we wondered if Renie was trying to contact us. In the years since she'd died, we never experienced any contact with her. And we didn't have any recollection of our lending her $50 or of her paying it back. It never occurred to us that the check might be a huge precognitive clue.

On the night of the festivities, Dennie told us she'd been hired to work with a detective in the cold case division. When she began describing the case and mentioned Greenacres, Trish suddenly blurted, "Is this the Christy Luna case?"

Dennie looked stunned. "How did you know?"

"You're not going to believe this." Rob walked over to the drawer where we'd put Renie's check, brought it out, and told the story of our involvement in the case through Renie. We realized we were the inadvertent connection in a series of events that led to a startling synchronicity and precognition. And it all revolved around the unsolved disappearance of Christy Luna, two psychics who didn't know each other, were separated by nearly a quarter of century, and yet worked on the case.

Interestingly, Dennie led the detective to the same wooded field where Renie had directed us all those years ago. Dennie said the body was buried somewhere in the undeveloped land. In 2009, the body still hadn't been found and case remained open.

Fast forward to August 2019, thirty-five years after her disappearance. Palm Beach County Sheriff Ric Bradshaw announced that his office had received what he believed was a credible tip about where the girl might be buried. He said a recent social media campaign designed to raise awareness and revive the case may have worked. "In May, the social media division put together a documentary, fortunately for us, the people that are out there paid attention to this and called us and gave us what we believe is one of the most credible leads that we have gotten to date to solve this case," said Sheriff Bradshaw.

Subsequently, anthropologists with Florida Gulf Coast University were enlisted to assist in the excavation of the site. Previously, the anthropology team excavated a prehistoric site not far from where Christy disappeared three decades ago. According to Dr. Heather Walsh-Haney, anthropologists studying skeletal remains can determine gender and age, how and when a person died. "We've identified human remains that have been buried for seven thousand years in Florida soils, so certainly our environment here is conducive to preservations," she said.

Detective William Springer, who has worked the case since 1984, said, "I've gone through a lot of good suspects and come out with nothing. This one, I don't build my hopes on. I like it, I think it's good lead, I'm going to follow through with it."

Unfortunately, after four days of digging, the only bones found were identified as animal remains. If the department is working with any psychics this time around, they weren't saying.

DANGERS OF TUNING IN

Working with police to find missing persons or solve crimes using your psychic abilities may sound like an exciting pastime, but that's *not* how many of the psychics we've talked to felt about it. Renie Wiley dreaded the psychic contact she made with killers. The dark energy she felt made her nauseous. One case in particular haunted her and she felt the killer's anger and hatred toward her. She continually invoked psychic protection and remained alert in her daily life for any possible threats coming her way.

Noreen Renier, like Wiley, is a psychometrist and has also experienced the gruesome horrors of murder as if she were the victim. In her book, *A Mind for Murder*, she describes holding a bloody dress while surrounded by eleven police officers. It was the first murder case she worked on. Initially, she felt as if she were about to throw up. She put the dress down and asked for a glass of wine. No wine was available, but she was given a shot of Scotch, which she said helped her relax and return to her work.

She picked up the dress again. She knew nothing about the case, except that the victim's name was Cindy and she had been murdered two days earlier. She began by describing a tall, slender woman in her mid-thirties. She saw a trailer and, in her mind, moved into it and into the kitchen.

"Suddenly, I was Cindy, and I felt a knife tearing repeatedly through the flesh of my back. It hurt! I moaned softly, then more urgently, as I felt the stabbing pains over and over again."

Then she was outside watching. "It was terrifying. I saw a man lean over Cindy and cut her throat, blood gushing out. As I watched her killer bend toward her lifeless body, my eyes snapped open. I was gasping. That was it. I'd had enough. I could not go on with this scene another moment. My heart was beating wildly."

CONNIE CANNON

Connie Cannon is another psychic detective who also has felt sickened by these contacts with dark energy emanating from criminal minds. She won't go on Facebook because she fears that one of the killers she tracked down might come after her. She won't even mention certain names so as not to attract further attention.

Her psychic detective work began with a dream that foretold a murder of someone close to her. With help from the police, she was able to prevent it.

"When we lived in Georgia and I was progressing through the degrees of magical skills at The House of Ravenwood, my Wiccan coven, my high priestess was named Lady Sintana. One night I sat bolt upright, wide awake in bed, and in the dresser mirror across from the end of our bed, an image began to play out."

In that wide-awake image, she saw Ravenwood, which was an old two-story Victorian home with lots of trees and shrubs in the front. It had a sidewalk leading up to steps that went to the front porch. "In the mirror I saw a short, bulky man with shoulder-length hair wearing a red plaid shirt walking up the sidewalk towards the porch. He was carrying a pistol that he held down beside his leg, and I knew he was planning to kill our high priestess. I glanced at the clock. It was exactly three-thirty am. Psychically, I knew it was going to occur the next night."

Early the next morning, Connie phoned Lady Sintana and described to her details of the waking vision. She called the police. They were no doubt dubious about dreams and premonitions, but just to be on the safe side, they put an officer on the property that night.

"Sure enough, at exactly three-thirty am, a short, bulky man with shoulder-length hair, wearing a red plaid shirt, walked onto the sidewalk approaching the porch to the house. The officer grabbed him. The man was a religious fanatic. He held a .38 in his hand, and he was intending to 'kill the witch.'"

After that, the Atlanta police occasionally used Connie on an on-call basis. She still gets visions, especially of catastrophic events like terrorist bombings, but she usually doesn't get enough information to enable her to do anything about it. She might see what's going to happen, but not precisely where or when.

Eventually, Connie had to give up her work with police because it was taking a toll on her. "Having that ability isn't one that I chose on a conscious level. Although I solved quite a few cases, especially missing children, it was brutal for me as a sensitive energy worker. I actually went through the experience with the missing children and young adults. It tore me up having to tell parents their child's circumstances."

HOW TO BECOME A PSYCHIC DETECTIVE

It's not a calling for the squeamish. It certainly requires the willingness to delve into some of the darkest hearts of humanity. At the same time, it requires a sense of compassion as well as integrity. You need to know the difference between guessing and intuitive messages or visions.

Beyond that, be clear about why you are getting involved. Is your primary interest gaining personal recognition or is it to provide help without concern for what you will gain from the experience? Investigators might quickly distinguish a true psychic from a publicity seeker.

What's needed now is for police officers, current or former, especially those who have worked with their hunches and "gut feelings," to be trained as psychic detectives.

In decades past, Renie Wiley and Noreen Renier led workshops to help authorities develop their intuitive skills. Well-qualified and case-tested psychics are the best ones to conduct such training.

The College of Policing in Great Britain, as mentioned earlier, has recommended that when a psychic offers help, investigators should take the offer seriously. American policing authorities should step forward, like the British, to recognize the value of people with psychic abilities. They should institute a training program to test and prepare volunteers from police departments or retired officers to work as psychic detectives. Such a program could be coordinated through psychic research organizations like the Institute of Noetic Sciences, Rhine Research Center, or the University of Virginia's Division of Perceptual Studies.

7

SHAMANIC VISIONS

"Shamanism is a path of knowledge, not of faith, and that knowledge cannot come from me or anyone else in this reality. To acquire that knowledge, including the knowledge of the reality of the spirits, it is necessary to step through the shaman's doorway and acquire empirical evidence."
—Michael Harner

Shamans are perceivers of visions, of mysterious phenomena manifested through rituals and ceremonies. While shamanism is commonly associated with tribal cultures in some distant mountains, jungle, or desert, everyone alive today is actually a descendant of shamanic practitioners. From the Druidic traditions in the British Isles to the Tungusic people of North Asia to the caves of Galilee in the Middle East, shamanism is the world's first mystical tradition. It belongs to everyone's heritage.

However, it's more about experience than faith, more about wisdom and self-mastery than belief. It's at least 10,000 years, dating back to the mystery schools of ancient Egypt, classical Greece and even earlier to hunter-gatherer cultures. Surviving traditional cultures have an unbroken link to shamanism, and for that reason the interest of Western people in the spiritual tradition has become a point of controversy.

For the past fifty years, a growing number of Westerners have begun exploring shamanism, usually through the window of these surviving traditional cultures where psychic phenomena is a central theme of life, not an outlier. Contrary to the concerns of some members of traditional cultures, many shamans have prophesized the expansion of shamanism into Western culture and see it as a positive act that ensures the continued pursuit of these ancient practices.

Shamans are considered the spiritual guides for their community. They move between matter and spirit, between form and energy. They are animists—meaning that through their experiences they have become convinced that everything that exists in this world is alive and has a spirit, including the earth, trees and rocks. According to shamans, we are spiritual beings manifested as humans. Our true home is elsewhere; our true essence is non-physical.

In addition, shamans say that these spiritual energies are all interconnected in a vast web of life. So anything that happens to one form of life affects the entire web. That's similar to Indra's net in Hindu mythology. It's said that one tug on the god Indra's net ripples throughout the universe.

Western spiritual seekers—especially those of us with heritage from the British Isles and Europe—are bearers of a broken tradition, whose shamanic roots were abolished by foreign invaders. Ancient sacred sites were destroyed and replaced with churches and monasteries. The ancient rituals honoring the Earth and the spirit in all things were banished and replaced by beliefs that emphasized an all-powerful male deity requiring faith and obedience. Because the link to our shamanic heritage was broken, Western people are generally unaware of our connection to the spirit world.

"In my opinion, it is unsafe not to know shamanism," writes Michael Harner in *Cave and Cosmos: Shamanic Encounters with Another Reality*. Harner, who is considered the godfather of neo-shamanism in the West, adds: "Virtually all humans have unconscious connections with spirits, but the vast majority of Westerners lack conscious knowledge of them and thus fail to employ them to help and protect themselves."

In spite of the worldwide effort of missionaries to abolish shamanism, some tribal cultures have managed to maintain and sustain a link with their ancient heritage. Among them are the

Q'ero Indians of Peru and the Kogis of Colombia, who fled high into the mountains at the time of the Spanish conquest, and were never converted by Christian missionaries. The Q'eros are now one of the leading forces in spreading knowledge of shamanism to the Western world. They do so through workshops led by Westerners trained by Q'eros.

Some of those American teachers also have sponsored visits by Q'eros. These workshops are directed at reconnecting Westerners to their own shamanic heritage, hence the practice is referred to as neo-shamanism. Such workshops can sometimes create a curious blend of cultural messages.

One December in the late 1990s, we attended a Q'ero healing ceremony, sponsored by the Four Winds Society, at a Unity Church in West Palm Beach that included several Q'ero shamans. They were seated on the floor of the stage, an audience in front of them, as they prepared an herbal mixture and chewed cocoa leaves. A few feet away was a ten-foot decorated Christmas tree, one of the primary symbols of Western religious culture. On this particular evening, instead of Christmas gifts, audience members who approached the stage received spiritual cleansing from the shamans.

Such cleansing rituals can provide a temporary sense of well-being, a cleansing of the soul. However, for individuals whose well-being has been seriously damaged and who feel that a part of them is missing, shamans can perform a deeper healing experience.

SOUL RETRIEVAL

One of the powers of the shamans is the ability to travel out of body and into the spirit world with the intent of retrieving a soul or spirit fragment that has become disconnected, trapped or lost, often times as a result of a dramatic or shocking incident or series of incidents. "Shamanic work can be compared to health care in modern times," writes Barbara Stevens Barnum in *Spirituality in Nursing: From Traditional to New Age.* "For example, soul retrieval closely resembles modern psychotherapy whereby the therapist seeks to find repressed portions of the client's personality. Like the psychiatrist, the shaman is very careful not to return a missing portion of 'soul' that has not been cleansed of its damage."

However, shamans emphasize that soul retrieval is only part of the process of healing and requires recipients to participate in the process, which may require changes in behavior and attitudes that affect emotional and physical well-being.

"If the other layers of the self aren't addressed, no spiritual healing approach can bring lasting results," writes Kelley Harrell, a shamanic teacher and author of *Teen Spirit Guide to Modern Shamanism: A Beginner's Map Charting an Ancient Path.* "We still have to address them along with soul retrieval and integration. We have to practice mindfulness. We may have to change our routine, our relationships or perhaps how we see ourselves. We have to be prepared to make whatever shift—small or great—is required of us to remain vitally empowered."

When Lauren Raines, a sculptor and artist, was going through a divorce, she heard about an energy healer and herbalist in Crownsville, Maryland. She was at a point in her life where she was "very open to anything," and went to him for a soul retrieval.

"He was very businesslike, and without knowing anything about me, put on his drums tape and headset, had me lie down next to him, and we tranced together. At the end of the session he blew soul fragments back into my body, and we talked about what he saw. We talked about cutting the cords from my ex-husband, and my former community that I'd left when I moved. He concluded the session by telling me: You'll know it's all over when you see a magenta flower that looks like a cosmos, and a terra cotta angel.'"

Eight months later, Lauren crossed the country with all her possessions and her cat loaded into her van. She was determined to move back to Berkeley, California, and start a new life. She had decided she would sleep in her van if necessary until she found somewhere to move.

"I began my adventure as soon as I arrived with a visit to a coffee house I last visited twenty years earlier. Almost immediately I was greeted by a long-ago friend, who recognized me, bought me a cup of coffee, and offered me a place to stay. I didn't have to spend a single night in my van, and when I walked into his living room there was a huge photograph of a magenta cosmos flower hanging above his fireplace."

A few months later, Lauren answered an ad for a roommate. "I walked into a house with an altar, and in the center of it was a terra cotta angel." She knew she'd found the right place, especially when she found out her new roommate was a colleague of Starhawk, a woman she admired. "Starhawk's writings were the foundation of my MFA thesis more than a decade earlier. Just like that, my new life began, and I ended up working with the very people I most wanted to work with, never having had to even try! The shaman was entirely right in his prediction."

The shaman gave her the signposts that would signal Lauren when her transitional period was finished. But Lauren had to act in a manner that completely changed her life in order to fulfill the promise of a new future. The appearance of the cosmos flower and terra cotta angel confirmed to her that she was on her way.

Shamans note that if you turn over your healing to another person, you are giving away your power. "Such seekers often desire to find a teacher who will act as an intermediary between themselves and the helping spirits—a trait that is more characteristic of our organized religions in which bureaucratized priesthoods stand between us and the sacred realms," writes Sandra Ingerman, a shaman and co-author with Hank Wesselman of *Awakening to the Spirit World: The Shamanic Path of Director Revelation.*

That's why shamans might require the recipients of healing energy to set out on a challenging journey aimed at self-discovery.

VISION QUEST

It's known as a vision or power quest, and is a trying experience that lasts for hours or days. These quests typically take place in wilderness areas, and are embarked upon to receive a significant vision, sometimes delivered by a power animal. In traditional cultures, boys and young men are sent out into the wilderness, often without food, water or shelter. Their quest is to seek spiritual guidance and direction for their lives through an encounter with a guardian animal, spirit guide or a force of nature. Shamans believe that spirits are more likely to provide assistance when the seeker is deprived of basic needs.

"Regardless of culture, it (the vision quest) commonly required seekers to prove themselves by suffering voluntarily, such as from fear, hunger, thirst, extreme cold or heat and exhaustion. In shamanism, suffering is not a method of atoning for one's 'sins,' but a way of attracting the help of powerful spirits," writes Michael Harner in *Cave and Cosmos: Shamanic Encounters with Another Reality.*

In his book, Harner describes a fascinating personal experience, a power quest in a cave, that required him to bring food. He carefully followed clues and guidelines provided by earlier researchers, anthropologist Walter Kline and ethnologist Williard Park. According to Park, rather than being deprived of sustenance, the shamans of the Paviotso (Northern Paiute) took food with them into caves for power quests that lasted a single night, and included a midnight meal that would help attract helpful spirits.

In his quest in the early 1980s, Harner entered a cave in the Shenandoah Valley of Virginia one evening. He brought a sleeping bag, sandwich and flashlight with him. But once he found his place deep within the cave, he turned off the flashlight and kept it off.

He didn't know if anything would come of his night in the cave. After all, he wasn't a descendant of Native American spirits and he didn't partake in any hallucinogenic plants or play drumming music commonly associated with entering a shamanic trance.

He asked the spirits to have compassion for him and provide him more power for his work in healing others. Following the guidelines he had read about, he settled into his sleeping bag. He would sleep until midnight, then wake up and eat his meal. After that, he would wait to see what happened.

Two minutes before midnight he was awakened by the caress of a wing against his cheek from a passing creature. He considered it a good sign. He sat up, ate his sandwich, and waited. He knew from an earlier vision quest in the Amazon that the spirits might attempt to frighten him. In the earlier experience, he was accompanied by Shuar Indian guides who protected him. Now he was alone, deep in the darkness of an enormous cave.

Nearly an hour passed in silent darkness when, he recalls: "Suddenly, from the direction of the distant entrance of the cavern, came the sound of hooves. The sound became louder, it was clearly the sound of animals. I could not believe what I was hearing."

The sound of galloping became so loud that Harner covered his ears and feared that he was about to be trampled. "Then the thundering hoofs swept past on both sides of me, rushing deeper in the cave and beyond.... 'We are horse,' they said, in a communication that was like telepathy, but stronger."

He felt ecstatic from the experience. He knew it wasn't a dream. He was wide awake. The cave turned quiet again. But the cave encounters were not over. "An immense and indescribable power" rushed toward him from the cave's entrance. "It swept overwhelmingly through my body like a freight train. A surge of immense energy filled my body. I was astonished. The power had come! Then the animal was gone." He felt awe and gratitude.

POWER PLACES

A quest for power requires a destination, a place that takes you away from your everyday life. That's why such quests often take place in deserts, mountains, or caves. Certain places are considered sacred by shamans, places where the spirits of native ancestors are said to dwell and are there to interact with descendants, and friends of the descendants who treat these sacred sites and their spirit inhabitants with respect.

One such power place is Canyon de Chelly in northeastern Arizona in the Four Corners region. The canyon is both a national monument and part of the Navajo Nation. Most people who visit the canyon only view it from parking areas on the rim. Access to the canyon is restricted, requiring a Navajo guide. Rob journeyed to Canyon de Chelly in 1992 for a four-day vision quest with a group led by Alberto Villoldo, founder of the Four Winds Society. Late one evening he found his personal power spot.

It was near midnight when he and the others climbed into the rocks, each of them in search of their personal power place. Under the light of the moon, Rob climbed over rocks and boulders higher and higher until he found the perfect resting place on a large flat rock. The temperature was in the upper thirties, but he tried to ignore the chilly air as he meditated and waited.

Nearly an hour passed and he had barely moved. He was drifting between wakefulness and a light sleep when a vivid vision came to him. He could see across the canyon where three Indians were walking along a perilous trail on the side of the rock wall. He could see them clearly, as if it were daylight, each with a cloth band wrapped around his forehead and tied at the back. Their long hair fell over their shoulders. The third one in line turned his head and stared back at him. To Rob's surprise, the man suddenly soared across the canyon, moving swiftly toward him. Rob jerked fully awake and the vision vanished.

The next morning, seated in a circle with several others, Rob related the vision. One of the men suggested that the Indian was not attempting to physically harm him, but to kill his ego. But Rob hadn't allowed him to do it. Had he failed at his vision quest? It seemed so, but another opportunity presented itself.

Just before leaving the canyon, Rob experienced one final vision. This time, while meditating on top of another boulder, a part of him was projected out of his body. As he soared away, he was aware of a powerful force sweeping through the canyon. He was ecstatic, free of his body. Where would he go, he wondered. What would he do?

A distant voice called out to him. He tried to ignore it, but the voice became more urgent. It was pulling him back to the boulder. He heard it again as his awareness returned fully to his body. He looked over his shoulder. Of course, they were leaving and the others were waiting in the van at the rim. They'd undergone long days of hiking through the canyon, setting up camp, followed by shamanic rituals that carried on late into the night. The combination resulted in an array of mystical experiences reported by the participants.

In Rob's case, his visions would have lasting effects. He would go on to write four novels with Native American and shamanic themes, one of which won an Edgar Allan Poe award and another that was a finalist for the award. Meditation would become a regular part his life, and as a meditation instructor, he would occasionally teach classes in shamanic meditations.

A few years prior to embarking on that vision quest, Rob had written a vision quest scene into the life of one of the most beloved movie characters—Indiana Jones. When he adapted the screenplay of *Indiana Jones and the Last Crusade* into a novel for LucasFilm and Ballantine Books, he included a flashback (not seen in the movie) in which Indy recalls a vision quest he embarked on at age eighteen. Under the guidance of a Navajo elder, Indy climbed to the top of a mesa. Alone and without food or water, he managed to build a shelter and waited. The old Navajo had told Indy that he must wait for an animal to approach him and from that time on it would be his protector and spiritual guardian.

Here's a brief excerpt:

Two days past, and his stomach was empty, his throat dry. He wanted more than anything to climb down and find water. He stood up and walked to the edge of the mesa and stared down. What had possessed him to do something so crazy?

Indy was about to start his descent when he thought he heard the voice of the old Indian telling him to wait. Startled, he turned around. No one was there. His hunger and thirst were causing him to hear voices, he thought. But instead of climbing down the mesa, he headed back to the shelter.

He had taken no more than a dozen steps when suddenly an eagle swooped out of the sky, skimming low over the flat, rocky surface. The majestic creature landed on the wall of his shelter. He had found his protector.

For some entering the realm of shamanism, a vision quest opens the gateway to shamanic journeys. Others are initiated into shamanism when they recover from a serious accident or illness, or a near-death experience. But you don't have to be a shaman to pursue these journeys. Unlike belief systems where a priest is the designated conveyer of the word of spirit, shamanism is accessible to all who seek.

While the preferred method is to work with a group of shamanic explorers, you can also practice on your own. There are numerous CDs available to both inform and guide you on a shamanic journey. Typically, they feature shamanic drumming, a steady, rapid monotonous beat that helps you move into a trancelike state.

PRACTICE: FINDING YOUR POWER ANIMAL

Shamans consider animal spirits to be powerful allies in their healing work and call on them frequently. They might beckon a variety of animals if the circumstances call for it, but usually they consider one species their power animal. If you are drawn to a particular animal—a dolphin, a jaguar, an eagle, whatever—then you might've already found your power animal. If not, try this meditation for uncovering your power animal.

When a power animal appears in a vision, you are encountering the archetype, soul, or essence of that animal, not an individual animal. The meaning associated with that animal should resonate with you. Think of the animal as a powerful ally, a guiding force.

Settle into your place for meditation, either sitting or lying on your back. Turn on your shamanic beat, as previously described. You might cover your eyes with a bandana or other eye cover.

Take a few deep breaths, relaxing your body from head to toe. When you're ready, imagine you're walking down a trail through a pristine setting in nature. Take a few moments to locate it. Maybe it's a place you've visited before.

Let the drumming move you into a deeper meditative state. Pay attention to each step you take. Is the ground soft and spongy or dry and rocky? Is the path gentle or rugged? After a time, you come to a large rock with an oval indentation. It looks like the perfect place to sit and rest.

Notice your surroundings. What time of day is it? Is the sun shining? Is it overcast? Warm or cool? Be aware of details. As you rest on your boulder, watch for any sign of animal life in your surroundings, either on the ground or in the trees. An animal might appear that seems curious about you. Greet the creature. Think of it as a new friend, your power animal, your guide and protector.

Stay in this place and enjoy your surroundings until the drumming slows, calling you back. Give thanks to any beings that appeared, any messages that were received. Retrace your steps along the path, and fully return to your ordinary awareness.

When you're back, consider what the animal means to you. For example, a bear might trigger thoughts of power and strength. But are there other attributes related to the animal? If you search online or in a book on animal totems, you might discover the essence of bear power is also about solitude, individuality, a seeker of visions.

JOURNEYING

Shamanic meditations are usually referred to as journeys, and often these journeys go into a higher world, a middle world, or a lower world. In these journeys, you might encounter spirit guides, who appear in human or animal form. These journeys provide us with a bridge between the spirit world and the everyday world.

Shamans interpret these worlds as places, even though the spirit world is everywhere and nowhere. That doesn't mean these worlds aren't real. Interestingly, all shamanic traditions around the globe describe these same three worlds—upper, middle and lower—and they say each of these worlds has many levels.

"For many, those first journeys fulfill a deep longing to connect, or reconnect as it were, with the unseen, that other belief systems or practices don't provide. In those early stages, journeying seems to provide answers to everything, and for that reason it can be addicting, even escapist if not done with care," wrote neo-shaman Kelley Harrell in a blog post on *Huffington Post.*

The spirit worlds of shamanism are a source of healing, power and information for those who explore these realms. The guides we encounter are the protective spirits, there to assist us. They are not interested in directing, domineering or controlling us.

Traditional cultures designated these spirit worlds in the distant past, long before recorded history, long before Christianity. The Lower World is not hell; the Upper World is not heaven. The Lower World is a place where you can meet archetypal or universal mythical beings, such as the trickster, the magician, the sage, and other spirits known through mythology. In a sense, the Lower World is a spiritual source for all of nature. Whatever creature—human or animal—that you encounter can serve as a spirit guide. The being might offer a message or answer a question.

The best way to begin is to locate your point of entry to the shamanic worlds. There are numerous possibilities. Here's one method of entering the Lower World. Turn on your recording of shamanic drumming.

PRACTICE: THE LOWER WORLD MEDITATION

Settle down into a place where you feel comfortable and won't be interrupted. Wear headphones or earbuds to enhance the shamanic drumming. Take your time moving into a relaxed state. Begin by taking several deep breaths. Let the drumming lead you into a relaxed trancelike state.

When you're ready, find a place in nature that appeals to you. Notice your surroundings. Find your way to a nearby stream and follow it. Keep walking until you realize that you are standing near the top of a waterfall that flows down into a pool. You can see the spray in the air forming a rainbow.

You notice flagstone steps going down along the edge of

the waterfall and you follow them. Now you see a path that goes behind the waterfall. You step inside the curtain of water and into a cavern. You see a tunnel ahead, and light coming from deep within the cavern. You walk toward it as the floor descends deeper and deeper into the earth.

You reach an opening and when you come out to the other side, you find yourself in another world, a place in nature with dramatic scenery, mountains and forest, lakes and rocks. It's as if you've entered a primordial version of earth. It feels different from the world you left. The landscape is vibrant and filled with life. Your senses take in the richness of this world, and you start to see the beings that inhabit the Lower World.

There's a large tree nearby with an enormous canopy and next to it is your guide. It could be a power animal or person, or a mythical character from ancient times. Approach the guide and greet the being. Pay attention to what happens on your journey, how you feel, any sensations you experience. You might receive a verbal message, but it might also come through events and scenery. Notice if it's day or night, or if the sun is out or hidden. What's the weather like? Notice how your guardian acts, and any smells, tastes, or sounds. It's all part of the message. Express your gratitude to the guide.

When the drumming slows down, it brings you back into your everyday world. You might write about your experience in a journal. It will help you remember and assist you in future journeys.

PRACTICE: THE UPPER WORLD MEDITATION

Years ago, we met a man in his early twenties who had been bitten by a coral snake and fell into a coma for a couple of days. When he recovered, he described a fantastic experience that felt more real than this life. He visited a majestic crystal city— an impossible city without foundations. He called it the most awesome place that anyone could ever visit, and he wanted to tell everyone he met about it. The people looked human, but they were more than human.

His experience sounded very similar to a journey to the

Upper World. Fortunately, you don't have to get bitten by a poisonous snake to travel there.

You can access the Upper World in shamanic meditation through a similar process you followed with the Lower World. Once you're relaxed, turn on your drumming accompaniment, and imagine yourself in a pristine environment in nature. Maybe it's a forest, on top of a mountain or a tranquil beach at the edge of the ocean. See it, smell the air, feel a gentle breeze, notice the lighting, and the time of day.

Instead of burrowing into the earth, you're going to rise into the sky by climbing a rope or ladder, floating off in a hot air balloon, soaring away on the wings of a large bird, or leaping from a high cliff. You continue rising higher and higher until you come to a region of fog. You pass through it, and on the other side you enter the Upper World.

You might find yourself in a crystal city or a city of clouds. Spirits in human form reside in this higher realm and serve as teachers for explorers who make the journey. They answer questions and help us develop spiritual knowledge and wisdom.

Here you'll meet a guide who will answer any questions. Remember, the advice you receive is something you can accept or reject. Consider it closely, but make sure it feels right before you act on what you've been told.

When the drumming slows, you can return to your place of meditation by the same means as you ascended. In your journal, note the date and describe your feelings and what you discovered on your journey.

PRACTICE: THE MIDDLE WORLD MEDITATION

The Middle World is a hidden aspect of our world. It's a realm where the spirits of all living things exist and where these spirits develop the ability to shift into physical form. It's also a place where thoughts easily manifest into reality. It's here where our unconscious minds create our collective reality, which includes plenty of undesirable conditions that come into our personal experience.

While the Middle World offers us the opportunity to create

harmony in our lives and attract what we want, it's also a place where spirits of the dead cling to Earth, and where negative energy resides. In spite of these hazards, you can visit this realm safely to improve your life. But it's important to focus on all things that are positive, and not on anything that would cause harm.

The Middle World is also the home of ancient nature spirits, including fairies, elves, dwarves, gnomes, mermaids and mermen, plant devas, elementary nature spirits, and the beings of fairy tales, dreams, and fantasies. These beings, which are considered mythical in our daily world, can assist you in bringing balance and harmony into your life.

An opportune time to explore the Middle World in meditation is when you are searching for a lost item or looking for information that can't be easily found in the everyday world of Google. You begin again by relaxing and entering a trance through the repetitive drumbeat. The process of entering the Middle World is similar to the one you followed for finding your way into the Lower World. However, to avoid confusion, it's a good idea to use a different means of entering the earth. For example, if you entered the Lower World through a cavern after ducking behind a waterfalls, you might reach the Middle World by descending through the hollow trunk of an ancient tree, diving into a deep pool of water or opening a secret trapdoor leading into the earth.

You pass through the tunnel into the Middle World where again you'll be met by a guide or guides. The guide will show you what it is you seek, and then you return the same way you entered. While the experience is still fresh in your mind, write down what you learned and how you felt about what happened.

8

MEDIUMS AND CHANNELERS

The channels of intuitive knowledge are opened according to the intensity of individual need.
—Jane Roberts

Hazel Burley sits on a couch in a small room filled with books, her eyes shut, head cocked to one side as if she's listening to something or someone. Or seeing something. Her breathing slows and beneath her lids, her eyes flick back and forth, as if she's dreaming. "They're showing me something—a man whose name begins with the letter J." She touched the side of her head. "He's on the other side. Something about his head."

She frowns. "Now there are two of them motioning to their heads." She opened her eyes and looked at Rob, sitting across from her. "Does this make any sense to you?"

Rob glances up from the pad of paper where he has been taking notes. He knows it's best not to provide a medium or psychic with any leads, but in this instance it makes sense to comment and clarify. "Yes. Very much so. I know two men, one's a friend, the other a cousin. Their names are Jay and John, and they both died of brain cancer within the past year."

Hazel had no way of knowing about the two deceased men, their names and the causes of their deaths. She didn't know she would be reading for Rob until he'd arrived an hour earlier. She's a medium who lives in the Spiritualist community of Cassadaga, Florida. She has visions and hears voices. She says she is guided by a consortium of spirits and has been doing this for more than thirty years.

Hazel began studying mediumship in her mid-twenties. Her mentor was Wilbur Hull, one of the town's most famous residents, a quadriplegic who read for clients from his bed. When she reads for a client, she begins by asking the person to give her five colors. She then tunes in on the colors, which enables her to hear the spirits who provide information about the client.

While colors start the process for Hazel, other mediums have their own methods for entering an altered state of consciousness. Edgar Cayce, the most documented psychic of the twentieth century, had to enter a trancelike state like sleep before he could read. He was often called the sleeping prophet, the name of Jess Stearn's biography about him, and rarely remembered what he said. His wife or secretary transcribed the readings. According to Edgar Cayce's Association for Research and Enlightenment, the organization created to preserve Cayce's readings, he conducted 14,306 of them in the course of his life.

The readings covered a vast array of topics—diet and health, reincarnation, Atlantis, holistic treatments for various conditions, spirituality, esoteric information, and numerous prophecies about the future of the planet. As Cayce's fame grew, the rich and the famous began consulting him. Among his most famous clients were Woodrow Wilson, Irving Berlin, and George Gershwin. Thomas Edison and Nikola Tesla supposedly consulted Cayce separately, but the A.R.E. doesn't have any documentation to that effect.

Yet, in *Edgar Cayce: An American Prophet*, by Sydney Kilpatrick, the author notes that Edison and Tesla received readings from Cayce in Bowling Green, Kentucky, where the two men were lecturing at the Bowling Green School of Business. As Kilpatrick writes, "Unfortunately, little is known about these meetings. No documentary evidence exists in the Edison or Tesla archives, and Cayce's date book and other records pertaining to the meetings were later destroyed in two separate fires at Cayce's photography studios in Bowling Green. Additional correspondence known to have existed between Cayce, Edison, and Tesla was also later destroyed by a well-meaning but short-sighted volunteer at the Edgar Cayce archive in Virginia Beach."

Whatever actually happened, it's fascinating that two brilliant men, who began as partners and eventually became rivals, consulted with Cayce at the same function.

In 1936, nine years before his death, Cayce had a prophetic dream about his next life. It provides a glimpse of what life may be like in the next century and is right in line with many of the predictions Cayce made about earth changes.

"I had been born again in 2100 A.D. in Nebraska. The sea apparently covered all of the western part of the country, as the city where I lived was on the coast. The family name was a strange one. At an early age as a child I declared myself to be Edgar Cayce who had lived 200 years before. Scientists, men with long beards, little hair, and thick glasses, were called in to observe me. They decided to visit the places where I said I had been born, lived, and worked in Kentucky, Alabama, New York, Michigan, and Virginia.

"Taking me with them the group of scientists visited these places in a long, cigar-shaped metal flying ship which moved at a high speed. Water covered part of Alabama. Norfolk, Virginia, had become an immense seaport. New York had been destroyed either by war or an immense earthquake and was being rebuilt. Industries were scattered over the countryside. Most of the houses were built of glass. Many records of my work as Edgar Cayce were discovered and collected. The group returned to Nebraska, taking the records with them to study…"

An interesting video and recording of Cayce on YouTube is from June 1939, where he talks about his work, the kinds of readings he does—health and "life reading" —and provides a general overview of his life. As a native of Kentucky, his voice holds a down home, Southern twang that conjures images of happy family gatherings. That voice is genuine.

On a fall evening twenty years later, Jane Roberts and her husband, artist Robert Butts, decided to try a Ouija board. After repeated attempts, someone named Seth came through. The information provided interested them, so they kept using the board. One night, Roberts realized she could hear Seth's answers to their questions before they were spelled out on the board and she began speaking for him.

Seth, as described in Chapter 4 (Future Knowing) described himself as "an energy essence no longer focused in physical existence." Twice a week until 1984, when Roberts died, she would settle into a chair for a Seth session. When she felt his arrival, she removed her glasses and began to speak as Seth while Butts transcribed the material. These sessions resulted in more than thirty books about the nature of reality.

The topics they discussed were sometimes light, sometimes personal and private, always profound and insightful. The books are dense and fascinating and when you read them, you sense the genuineness of Seth's voice. After Roberts's death in 1984, her husband eventually published the "private" sessions. Much of the material deals with Roberts's struggle with rheumatoid arthritis and other personal details of their lives at the time. Even though she and Cayce both lived before the advent of YouTube and social media, some videos and audio recordings can be found on YouTube.

The videos of Roberts speaking as Seth (see Resources at the end of the book) are startling and strange even if you're familiar with the Seth material. She isn't wearing her glasses, that's the first thing you notice. Her eyes are larger, darker, and when Seth begins to speak, it's certainly seems that another personality is in charge. His voice is distinct, heavily accented, and he makes animated hand gestures as he rocks back and forth in the rocker where Roberts is sitting.

On that evening in 1963, Roberts entered an altered state of consciousness and wrote what she refers to as a "script" entitled "The Physical Universe as Idea Construction." She doesn't remember writing it and as soon as she returned to her own consciousness, she read it as if seeing it for the first time.

She had just finished her first science fiction novel and was casting around for an idea for her next book. The material she'd written in the script was foreign to her. It marked the beginning of her long journey with Seth.

At this point, you may be thinking that Hazel, Cayce and Roberts are/were professional mediums and channelers, but what about, well, *ordinary* people who have these experiences?

What about the parent, child, teacher, bus driver, writer, scientist, attorney, or artist who tune into stuff the rest of don't? What about you?

If you experience incidents in which you have impressions, see visions, hear voices, or receive information that's clearly outside of your norm, you may not have any desire whatsoever to turn pro. You may just want to understand what's happening to you. And then you may decide to nurture and develop this ability just to see where it will take you. If so, here are some techniques that should help in that development.

Meditation. A good place to start. It can be as formal as a class or as informal as taking a long walk in nature. It depends on your personality.

Some people are natural meditators. They can sit for a prescribed period of time every day at the same time, so that meditation simply becomes part of their routine. Other people don't want to sit still for fifteen or twenty minutes a day, and are more likely to take that daily walk, when nature performs its magic and their senses open up.

Rob, a yoga and meditation teacher, provides different techniques for the restless types in his book *Jewel in the Lotus*.

Mitch Horowitz, author of *The Miracle Club: How Thoughts Become Reality*, believes that meditation is essential for anyone on a spiritual journey. "...meditation provides a kind of foundational starting point to ensure the best mental and emotional state of prayer and the use of mind therapeutics."

Through meditation, author Whitley Strieber was able to communicate with his dead wife, Anne, and together they wrote *The Afterlife Revolution*.

Joe Dispenza, author of *You Are the Placebo: Making Your Mind Matter*, healed himself of a severe spinal injury by meditating four hours a day while confined to a friend's couch. After ten weeks, he was able to walk normally despite the fact that surgeons told him that without surgery, he wouldn't walk again.

Meditation proved to be vital in the development of mediumistic skills for author and public speaker Esther Hicks, who channels a consortium of souls known as Abraham.

The trick is to find the type of meditation that works for you and do it regularly

Awareness and receptivity. These qualities are intrinsic to the development of any skill, but are particularly important for the development of psychic ability. They're predicated on one word: belief. If you *believe* such abilities are possible, if you *believe* that what you experienced is true, if you *believe* it's important for you to develop and nurture these skills, then you're already aware and receptive. Now toss in a desire that's so emotionally powerful it could move mountains and you're on your way!

Synchronicity. In this journey, meaningful coincidence is your greatest ally. When you're really focused and psyched about what you're doing and feel it as a burning in your belly, synchronicities flourish. They provide direction, confirmation, warnings, comfort. You'll recognize it when it happens. You may call it by a different name—the flow, God winks, WTF, the universe shouting. But, bottom line, it's Carl Jung's synchronicity waving its arms and shouting, *Yeah, go for it*!

CONSULTING A MEDIUM

Even people who don't believe in an afterlife or the paranormal sometimes consult a medium when they've lost a loved one. The best way to choose a medium is through a referral from someone who has had a reading with the individual. If that's not possible, then the Internet can be a terrific resource.

These days, many psychics and mediums have websites and are on Facebook, Instagram, and other social media. Instagram seems to be particularly popular. Thanks to hashtags, it's easy for psychics to advertise themselves and their work. If they provide a testimonial page, read through what their clients say about them. Don't make your choice based just on their number of followers. It's inexpensive to buy followers on Instagram and a lot of people do it. The more followers you have, the more important you look and the greater the possibility that you can refer to yourself as "an influencer."

Psychic medium John Edward, for instance, has more than 57,000 followers as of September 2019. James van Praagh, another author and medium, has more than 47,000 followers. Their brand is psychic mediumship. However, there are psychic mediums who are equally talented but don't have TV shows, podcasts, radio programs, and don't demand hefty fees for readings, workshops, and speaking engagements.

Psychic mediums, as a mean of comparison, have far fewer followers than, say, Stephen King, who has 1.1 million followers and is following just one person, which isn't even a person, but a movie—*IT*, from his own book. J.K. Rowling is so popular worldwide that she has dozens of Instagram accounts under that name and using her photo.

The point here is that you can find a reputable psychic medium by using your intuition. And sometimes, synchronicity sweeps in and helps you out.

THE ANIMAL COMMUNICATOR

One June afternoon in 2016, our daughter, Megan, fell in love with a little gray and white puff of a kitten her friend Denise brought over to her house. The kitten was the runt of her litter, had wise eyes and an energy you could feel in your heart. Megan adopted her and named her Piper.

Piper's first friend was Nika, Megan's dog. They preened each other, played, chased each other around the house. When Megan visited us on weekends, with both Piper and Nika, Piper won over our dogs, Noah and Nigel, both of them large Golden Retrievers. The dogs preened her, loved on her, and she ate it up. When Megan began watching dogs in her home, Piper accommodated them. She stood up to the bullies and stared down the little yappers until they skulked away, probably ashamed of themselves. When Piper spent time here with us, she explored our back yard, chased lizards, climbed trees, did all those cat things but with a certain grace and finesse.

On October 28, 2018, Megan returned home from a movie with Denise and they found Piper dead on the living room floor. Megan, hysterical, thought one of the dogs she was watching had killed her. But a veterinarian who arrived shortly afterward to pick up her dog saw that Megan was distressed and examined Piper. She said there were no bite marks, that it was likely Piper died of a heart attack, that she'd had some sort of congenital weakness.

But they couldn't figure out why Piper's fur was so damp and why things on Megan's dresser, where Piper often sat, peering out the window, had been knocked to the floor.

Megan was distraught. She thought she could have done something to prevent Piper's death, and continued to blame herself.

Several weeks later, Megan discovered an animal communicator, Heather Bristol. It turned out that Megan used to ride Heather's horse years earlier before Heather became a medium. Since Heather lived close by, Megan booked a thirty-minute session.

By the day of the reading, Megan was pretty sure that Piper had died on her dresser. But she was still puzzled by why her body had been in the living room, her fur soaked.

Heather told Megan that Piper had died of an aneurysm while on the dresser and had fallen to the floor. The several dogs in the house, including Nika, had brought Piper's body out into the living room and tried to revive her by nudging and licking her repeatedly. That accounted for her wet fur.

According to Heather, Piper's previous past life had been long and happy, but her death had been planned—i.e. she'd been put down for some old age complication. Her soul had chosen to return for a short, happy life in which she died a natural death. This information suggested that animals have spiritual agendas and reincarnate with intention, just as we do, and helped soothe Megan's sadness.

Heather noted that Piper had been around the house, something Megan already knew because she'd seen her, darting along the kitchen counter as she often had when she was alive to position herself in the window in front of the sink. Megan said she felt Piper had come into her life to teach her that death isn't the end, and her reading confirmed that.

Heather also said that Piper would be back and that even if her return wasn't as a cat, Megan would recognize her.

This reading was enormously healing for Megan and she subsequently signed up for classes with Heather to develop her own mediumistic skills. Not surprisingly, these events had a number of accompanying synchronicities.

Denise, who had given Piper to Megan, was with her when she got back from the movie. Denise actually spotted Piper's body first and stayed with Megan for a long time in the aftermath. The next day, October 29, National Cat Day, Megan buried Piper and Denise called her, hysterical because she'd found the cat she'd rescued dead on her porch. The cat had been hit by a driver who had left her a note of apology and placed her cat on the porch. Megan went over to Denise's to comfort and console her and to bury her cat. While she was doing that, she found out that another friend had to put down his cat. On National Cat Day.

Synchronicities occur more frequently during pivotal life events. If nothing else, the startling odds involved force us to pay attention. These seemed to be telling Megan that death isn't the end, that at some level we're all connected, and the medium became the voice of those messages.

Mediums and channelers are the human expression of psychic energy. But this energy also finds a collective expression in events so weird and startling that everyone involved is affected. This weird manifestation involves shoes and happened to Sharon Catley of Canada.

THE TRAVELING SHOES

For thirty-three years, Sharon worked at a marine transportation company. During that time she was moved into several different office locations within the same building. Her department consisted of three offices—hers, that of a co-worker, and a large foyer that was used for storage.

"One of the things that were stored in that room were special safety shoes. They were made of rubber and were like galoshes with steel toes that you could put over your regular shoes to enter areas of our location that required additional safety," Sharon wrote. "There were about ten pairs in various sizes and colors. We would laugh because they looked a bit like clown shoes. Anyway, every morning when we came into work, the shoes which had been stored on a two-level shelf would be all over the floor. They stayed in place on the shelves all day but every morning they were off the shelf."

One morning, Sharon arrived at work and the payroll lady came in to talk to her before she'd had a chance to pick up the shoes. She asked what the shoes were doing all over the floor and Sharon told her the story. "She was of Asian descent and said that in that culture this would be the sign of a ghost and that shoes in the house are considered bad luck."

The shoes continued to jump off onto the floor for the next few years until it was decided to do a rearrangement of the storage foyer. The shelf with the shoes was placed at the opposite end of the room and, for some reason, the shoes suddenly ceased their nightly wandering.

"We had done quite a thorough investigation before to see what the cause for this movement might be (breezes or being moved by the night janitor but he did not come every night). We later learned that the ashes of a former employee had been stored where the shelves were originally located. The urn had been brought to facilitate the scattering of the ashes at sea but had been forgotten behind some boxes for many years. It had been found and removed just before we and the shoes moved into those offices."

Sharon and the payroll lady concluded that the ghost of the person whose ashes had been left there felt disrespected by them for placing the stinky shoes in that area. The urn had stayed in the storage room for so many years, essentially forgotten, the ghost's displeasure was compounded by the fact that its ashes should have been floating freely in the Pacific Ocean. "It expressed its displeasure by tossing the shoes around," Sharon wrote in a follow up email. "The shoes have since been moved into a closet just outside these offices and are still behaving themselves. There have been no reports of mysterious activity in the storage room so the ghost must finally be at peace."

When you really think about it, the entire traveling shoes episode is curious, eerie, and could be written off as some sort of Fortean anomaly that challenges the boundaries of reality. But it happened repeatedly, with regularity, until the shelf was moved. This fact lends credence to the idea that it was the manifestation of the energy, the consciousness, of a dead person who apparently was irked that his ashes had been stuffed into a storage area and forgotten.

Sometimes, the medium is simply the person who—like the payroll woman—identifies what might be going on.

MEDIUM VS. PSYCHIC

A medium or channeler interacts/communicates with the spirits of the dead and those spirts provide information about the past, present, future. The mediums are like intermediaries between you and the spirits.

A psychic reads your personal energy through a highly developed and enhanced intuition. There's no intermediary.

Both mediums and psychics may use tools like Hazel's colors or they may use cards, a personal item, a birthdate. Or they may not use anything at all.

But at times, some psychics who don't consider themselves to be mediums do have interactions with the spirits of the dead. They don't intentionally head out into some etheric place looking for the spirits. Instead, the spirits insert themselves into the psychic's awareness. Millie Gemondo of West Virginia is one such psychic.

MILLIE GEMONDO

We've known Millie since August 1992 and were introduced to her by our accountant, who is from the same West Virginia town. The night before Hurricane Andrew was supposed to hit South Florida, Trish had her first phone reading with her and was impressed. One of the things Millie told her was that in spite of what the National Hurricane Center was predicting, we wouldn't be hit by Andrew. The area of impact would be much smaller than the tri-county area that comprised the South Florida peninsula.

It was a relief to hear it would miss us, but we had prepared earlier in the day with food and supplies, hurricane shutters, extra batteries for flashlights. Millie was right. Hurricane Andrew was a no-show in Palm Beach County, but demolished Homestead and parts of Miami. It wasn't until Dan Rather flew to Homestead that the world got its first look at the utter devastation.

Other readings over the years proved to be equally accurate. She visited us in the late 1990s, when Trish's mother, Rose Marie, was in an Alzheimer's unit, and one afternoon they drove over to the facility to see her. A common manifestation of Rose Marie's illness was that she often claimed her brothers and sisters—four of them, all deceased—had stopped by to see how she was doing. Trish never reminded her they had all passed on years ago. Instead, she asked how they were and listened to her stories about their visits.

On this particular day, Trish and Millie found Rose Marie in her room, looking for her shoes. She was excited to see them and immediately told them that her sister and brother had visited. Millie didn't know anything about Rose Marie's siblings, but suddenly said, "Is your brother's name Dick?"

Rose Marie's eyes lit up. "Yes, he's my baby brother."

"He's sitting there at the foot of your bed."

"Yes!" Rose Marie exclaimed.

"You can see him?" Trish asked when her mother had gone into the bathroom.

"He's gone now. But yes, I could see him."

From then on, whenever Rose Marie told us a dead relative had visited her, we believed her.

So even though Millie doesn't refer to herself as a medium, she can see spirits when their presence is strong.

PREPARING FOR A READING

When you're having a reading with a medium or a psychic, there are some simple tips to follow to ensure the information isn't tainted by anything you say or share with the person doing the reading.

Good psychics don't ask you why you want a reading. They don't fish for information.

Kathy Adams, a Cassadaga psychic whose specialty is psychometry, asks for a personal object, preferably a piece of jewelry or something else that you wear, which she then reads. But Kathy can actually read anything. When Megan sees her, Kathy reads her cell phone, since Megan—like many of us-is closely attached to her phone. The idea is that any object will do as long as your energy is part of it.

During our research for *Aliens in the Backyard: UFOs, Abductions, and Synchronicity,* we asked Kathy to read a vial of holy water, which a Canadian man had been carrying for months after he had a strange UFO encounter in his back yard. We didn't tell her what the vial contained or anything else about why we asked her to read it. And Kathy, an ex-ER nurse, thought it was filled with urine! She read the vial anyway and correctly described what had happened to the man.

Don't sit like the proverbial bump on a log during the reading, arms folded across your chest, your mouth zipped shut.

If you're physically closed, then you're also closed vibrationally, emotionally, and it's more difficult for the psychic to read anything about you.

Sometimes, a psychic will be delivering information and will pause to ask you if it resonates. It's fine to confirm or deny. This helps the psychic adjust the information received. In a recent reading, Kathy described a spirit she saw around Trish— an older gentleman, bald, hunched shoulders, blue eyes—and asked if she recognized who she was describing. Trish said she did, that it was her dad. The confirmation told Kathy she was on the right track.

During another reading, Kathy mentioned the spirit of a middle-aged woman who was around Trish. She described the woman and asked if Trish had any idea who she might be. Initially, she didn't. She later realized Kathy had described her former editor, Kate Duffy, who died in 2009.

Kathy says that she sees spirits when "they want to be known." So it seems that the dead, like the living, have intentions and desires that facilitate their appearance.

If you go into a reading as a skeptic, it's likely you'll leave as a skeptic.

This important point can't be overemphasized. Belief is the foundation of everything we experience. If you start your search for a psychic with the belief they're all frauds, then you'll probably select a fraud for a reading and come away from it with that belief confirmed. But if you believe that some people are psychically gifted, can communicate with the dead, can glean information from an object, then you might have a powerful experience with a psychic or medium.

We live in a complex matrix that is more than what our five senses perceive. Once we allow ourselves to open up, to receive, that matrix explodes open.

9

THE PHENOMENA OF NUMBERS

"When you have mastered numbers, you will in fact no longer be reading numbers, any more than you read words when you read books. You will be reading meanings."
—W.E.B. DuBois

In 2011, a Google search for 11:11 yielded 200 million links. Seven years later, in 2018, the same query brought back 472 million. In August 2019, that figure stood at 781 million. There may be various reasons for this figure leaping by 309 million in a single year or 581 million in eight years. But one explanation is *collective awareness* that 11:11 is significant in some way.

Carl Jung experienced many numerical synchronicities throughout his life and believed that numbers represent "an archetype of order which has become conscious." In other words, the particular pattern symbolized by the repetitive numbers is significant in the psyche of the person who experiences them. Once the message is deciphered, the pattern is no longer prevalent inside you and may not be noticed at all.

The tricky thing with the phenomena of numbers is figuring out what they mean for you. Among those hundreds of millions of links for 11:11 are countless explanations and definitions, but the only meaning that matters is the one you figure out for yourself. By interpreting them as metaphors, doing some research, and using your intuition, you can gain clarity and a deeper appreciation for how your inner self, your unconscious, guides you.

The number clusters can involve any repetitive numbers, but let's start with 1, 11, 111, 1111.

1, 11, 111, 1111

Uri Geller, the Israeli psychic, has a large area on his website about 11:11. He claims he started experiencing this number phenomenon in 1986, long before the Internet and social media. As his experiences proliferated, he began noticing the numbers on hotel room doors, microwave ovens, cars, documents, everywhere and anywhere.

When he finally wrote about it on his website, he was deluged with email from people who were experiencing the 11:11 phenomenon. He considers the numbers a "crack between two worlds...a bridge which has the inherent potential of linking together two very different spirals of energy."

Let's take a look at how 11s are connected to 9-11:

1) New York City has 11 letters
2) Afghanistan has 11 letters.
3) George W Bush has 11 letters.
4) New York is the 11th state.
5) The Twin Towers formed the number 11.
6) The first plane crashing into the Twin Towers was flight number 11.
7) Flight 11 was carrying 92 passengers. 9 + 2 = 11
8) The tragedy was on September 11, or 9/11 as it is known. 9+1+1=11
9) The date is equal to the U.S. emergency services telephone number 911: 9+1+1=11.
10) The total number of victims inside all the hijacked planes was 254. 2+5+4=11.
11) September 11 is day number 254 of the calendar year. Again 2+5+4=11.
12) The Madrid bombing took place on 3/11/2004. 3+1+1+2+4 =11.
13) The tragedy of Madrid happened 911 days after the Twin Towers incident.

This mind-boggling list suggests that some sort of internal order is at work here.

The meanings of the 11 phenomena range from illumination and enlightenment to protection by angels and spirit guides to confirmations, warnings, being ushered into a greater reality, the energy of something flowing in, being on the right path, in the right place, at the right time. Again, though, the significance should be *personal*, should resonate for you.

In 2009, author Nancy Pickard was promoting her novel *The Virgin of Small Plains* and emailed us that she had just finished a tour of 11 libraries, in 11 towns, in 11 days. "I guess I'm doing exactly what I'm supposed to be doing."

In June 2011, we were traveling in Costa Rica with our daughter, Megan. One morning in the town of Santa Elena, where the big draw is ziplining, Rob found a yoga studio owned by some American ex-pats and decided to take a class. While he was doing that, Trish and Megan went shopping. That area boasts a number of artists and they found some fantastic shops that featured local art, jewelry, sculptures. In a shop called Luna Azul, they did some serious shopping, took their purchases up to the counter, and the young clerk began her tally on a hand calculator.

As she did that, Trish was thinking of how much her parents, both deceased, had raved about their trip to Costa Rica years earlier, and knew her mom would have loved this particular shop. So much color, so many beautiful pieces of art to touch and appreciate. And then the clerk said, "Uh-oh. I made a mistake." She turned her calculator so they could see what she was talking about. "I punched in too many ones."

Trish and Megan just stared at the five ones: $111.11. Then they burst out laughing.

"Wow," Trish breathed.

"Awesome," Megan remarked.

"I'm so sorry," the woman said.

"Don't be," Trish told her. "This is a powerful number."

She glanced up, frowning. "Really?"

"Absolutely." Trish handed her a credit card.

"The actual price is $111.00," the woman explained.

Trish snapped photos of both receipts and later, in retrospect, realized she'd been thinking of her parents when the woman was tallying their purchases. From then on, one of the meanings of 11s and its various permutations, at least for her, was spirit contact.

Sometimes, 1111 gets very personal. In June 2018, Melissa and her husband, Jon, had to have their cat, Star, put down. She was nearly 21. When the vet went to their house to help her along, Melissa and John were playing an Azure Ray song, "November," which was her favorite song and made her more comfortable. As Melissa explains, "She was asthmatic and had anxiety and we would put that record on and it would soothe her. Star loved the song.

"Six months to the day that she left us (she left 6/6/2018 and this happened on 12/6/2018), I was thinking about her and for some reason happened to google the Azure Ray site and noticed that there was going to be a show in Brooklyn. It was a sign from Star. An Xmas ornament fell off the tree that evening—a star ornament, if I remember correctly."

Melissa often notices 11 or 11:11 or 1:11 on her phone's screen saver, and she saw it that afternoon when she learned about the Azure Ray concert at a small venue in Brooklyn. Jon also noticed it on the microwave. "So our cat sent us to a concert and on January 19, 2019, we went to the show."

A few days before the concert, Melissa messaged the band and asked them to play their song, "November". "When the band came out, Jon reached in his pocket. He had brought one of Star's toys with him to the show. They did play the song and I cried the whole time. At the end of the night, as I was going home, I looked at my phone. 11:11 PM."

These 11s can also be archetypal tricksters that seem to be poking fun at us. One day while researching 11 number clusters, Rob took a break to pick up our Mazda, which had gotten a new alternator. As he drove away from the garage, he glanced at his watch. The time read 3:17 PM. But when he glanced at the dashboard clock, he started laughing. The battery had been disconnected during the installation of the alternator, so the clock had stopped. It read: 11:11.

Earlier that same day, we had received a bill from our daughter's college for the year-end cleaning of the dorm suite she shared with three other women: $111 and loose change. If it indicated a flow of money, the joke was on us because the money was going out, not coming in.

Once you become aware of number phenomena, particularly that of 11s, you tend to notice them more frequently. It's as if you've become attuned to that archetypal energy. But with any number cluster, the question remains: are we being offered a glimpse into the internal symmetry and order of the universe? Are we peering into what physicist David Bohm called the implicate order, out of which everything else unfolds?

Pythagoras, the mathematician who lived around 500 B.C., believed that numbers constituted the fabric of the universe. For Jung, the number 1 was much more than just a number. In his autobiography *Memories, Dreams, Reflections*, he referred to it as a unity. "...not a number but a philosophical concept, an archetype and the attribute of God, the monad."

Regardless, it's a wake-up call. When it happens to you repeatedly, you can't help but sit up, pay attention, and then try to figure it all out. Sometimes, these number phenomena occur over a period of years and even prominent individuals who aren't psychics or mystics or writers delving into this bewildering soup take notice. Just ask former MSNBC anchor Keith Olbermann.

On bat night at Yankee Stadium in 2009, Yankee Brett Gardner swung at a pitch. His bat slipped out of his hands, sailed into the stands, and hit a kid, Jacob Smith, Olbermann's nephew. Nine years earlier, Yankee second baseman Chuck Knoblauch hurled a ball to first base. It bounced off the roof of the dugout and struck Marie Olbermann, Keith's mother. At the time, Olbermann was a sportscaster, covering baseball for Fox News. Knoblauch and Gardner both wore number 11.

Just think for a moment about the *odds* on that one. Look at what had to fall into place. Olbermann's mother and nephew were in Yankee stadium nine years apart, both of them hit during their respective games, Marie by a ball, Jacob by a bat— by players who both wore number 11. And, oh, at the time

Olbermann covered baseball for Fox News.

You hear stuff like this and invariably wonder who orchestrates it all. "Spontaneous order arises in living systems, from the atom to the galaxy," writes Dawson Church in *Mind to Matter*. But does the living system of baseball and sportscasters have its own peculiar order? Do artists and writers? Accountants? Engineers? Teachers? Do numbers?

HISTORICAL 11S

Take a look at these:

The WWI armistice was signed at 11:11 AM on the 11th day of the 11th month.

JFK was assassinated on 11/22.

The Mayan calendar ended at 11:11 universal time in 2012.

The U.S. Navy listed the 2012 solstice for 12/21/12 at 11

The Berlin Wall fell on 11/11/89

Yassar Arafat died on 11/11/04

At 11 AM on 11/11/1811, Cartagena, Colombia, became the second city in South America to declare its independence from Spain.

By 11-11-11, there had been so much hype about 11s that the awareness of the numbers had spread worldwide and resulted in some interesting news stories:

Egypt briefly closed the Great Pyramid on that day because of rumors that it was going to be used for ceremonies celebrating 11-11-11.

USA Today reported, "A lineup of digits at 11 minutes past the 11th hour on 11/11/2011 marks a moment that won't repeat for 100 years.

In Las Vegas, 3,200 marriage licenses were issued for 11-11-11, three times the usual amount. According to the county clerk, there hadn't been anything like that since 7-7-07, when 4,333 licenses were issued.

At 11:11 on 11-11-11, Veteran's Day, a boy was born to parents whose mother is an Air Force veteran and whose father is currently serving in the Air Force.

On a personal level, there were also some stunners. Sharlie, a poet, emailed us that at 11 AM on 11-11-11, she and her husband "joined to pray for health, prosperity, and safety. No small wish." After that, they went for a ride and he was joking about what he considered their superstitious behavior. *"And then a car pulled in front of us with the license place 1 1 1. It pretty much said it all."*

On that date, we found out that the foreign rights to one of our synchronicity books, *The 7 Secrets of Synchronicity*, had sold to Russia.

But what about other numbers? How far does this phenomenon go, anyway? Let's ask Judi Hertling.

JUDI'S RECORDS

For more than two years, Judi Hertling, a Canadian, has been tracking the repetitive number clusters that crop up in her daily life. The numbers, she said, showed up everywhere—on clocks, receipts, TV, magazines etc.—and are usually linked with terror-related events around the world. "The event appears to happen within four days of numbers appearing repetitively. Is this a universal warning for sensitives to send more light into the world?" she asks. "Or something else?"

That something else could be that the repetitive numbers are related to planetary empaths, individuals who are so sensitive to man-made and natural disasters they feel physical symptoms and a pervasive sadness. For Judi, the numbers may be the way her unconscious spares her the physical pain of these symptoms, which range from nose bleeds and migraines, heart palpitations to fever.

She has dozens of such examples now and has discovered a pattern: these incidents always occur within three to four days of a mass event, a natural or man-made disaster covered so extensively by the media that you would have to be living under a rock to miss it.

Here's her record:

2015

Nov 11, 12, & 13: 12:22, 10:10, 11:11, 12:12, 1:11, 2,22, 4:44, 555, 10:10, 1:11 , 2:22 (repeating over 3 days prior to event)

Nov 13, 2015 Event: Paris Attack. 3 Suicide bombers struck outside the State de France during a football match, then several mass shootings and a suicide bombing took place at cafes and restaurants, then the perps carried out another mass shooting and took hostages at an Eagles of Death Metal concert in the Bataclan theater. 130 killed, 413 people injured, 100 seriously injured. 7 attackers also died.

Nov 30, Dec 1/2015: 11:11, 2:22, 3:33, 11:11, 12:12, 4:44.

Dec 2, 2015 Event: Mass Shooting in San Bernardino, California. Mass shooting and attempted bombing at Inland Regional Center in San Bernardino at a Department of Public Health training event. 14 killed, 22 injured, 2 perps killed.

2016

March 19, 2016: 10:10, 11:11, 3:33, 4:44, 5:55, 12:12. 1:11

March 22, 2016 Event: Belgium bombing, Brussels airport and Maelbeek metro station 35 killed (including perpetrators) and more than 300 injured

July 6, 2016: 11:11, 1:11, 3:33, 5:55, 10:10, 11:11. 1:11. 222.

July 7, 2016 Event: Dallas shootings of police officers during a demonstration against police brutality. 5 police officers died, 7 officers and 2 civilians were wounded, perpetrator killed with an explosive delivered by a remote-controlled robot.

July 13, 2016: 10:10, 11:11, 1:11, 3:33, 4:44, 12:12, 12:22, 111

July 14, 2016 Event: Nice, France attack. A 19-ton cargo truck (2,240 pounds) was deliberately driven into crowds of people celebrating Bastille Day on the Promenade des Anglais. 86 people killed, 458 injured. Perpetrator killed.

July 20, 2016: 11:11, 3:33, 4:44, 10:10, 12:12, 111, 222, 11:11

July 22, 2016 Event: Munich attack at McDonald's restaurant near the Olympia shopping mall in the Moosach district of Munch, Germany. 10 (including perpetrator) killed, 36 injured.

2017

Sept 30 & Oct 1, 2017: 10:10, 11:11, 12:12, 1:11, 333, 444, 5:55, 11:11, 12:12,

2:22, 12:22, 1:11. (Repeating over 2 days prior to the event).

October 1, 2017 Event: Shooting Las Vegas. Lone gunman fired more than 1,100 rounds into opens fire at concert goers at Harvest Music Festival on the Las Vegas Strip. Perp died of self-inflicted gunshot wound. 58 killed, 851 injured. Deadliest mass shooting by an individual in the U.S.

October 29 & 30, 2017: 10:10: 11:11, 1:11, 3:33, 5:55, 10:10, 11:11, 1:11.

October 31, 2017 Event: Terrorist drives rental truck into cyclists and pedestrians along Hudson River in Manhattan. 8 killed, 11 injured, perp killed by police officers.

Nov 4, 2017: 11:11, 1:11, 3:33, 5:55, 10:10, 12:12, 1:11, 5:55

Nov. 5, 2017 Event: Mass shooting at First Baptist Church in Sutherland Springs, Texas. 26 killed, 20 injured. Deadliest shooting in Texas and fifth-deadliest shooting in the U.S. Perp died of multiple gunshot wounds and self-inflicted head injury.

Nov 20-21 2017: 222, 333, 444, 11:11, 12:12, 1:11, 3:33, 5:55. (repeating over 2 days)

Nov 24, 2017 Event: Terror attack in Egypt. Militants detonated a bomb inside a mosque in the Sinai Peninsula, then sprayed gunfire on panicked worshipers as they fled. 306 killed, 128 injured. Deadliest terrorist attack in Egypt's modern history. From the Washington Post: *"Survivors and officials described five pickup trucks carrying up to 30 gunmen—some of them masked—converging on al-Rawda mosque as the imam began his sermon. Some worshipers died in a suicide blast; others were gunned down as they ran. The attackers would later walk among the fallen, 27 of them children, shooting those who appeared to be breathing."*

Nov 25 -26, 2017: 333, 444,10:10, 12:12, 3:33, 5:55, 10:10, 1111, 12:22

Nov 27, 2017 Event: Terrorist Attack Iraq. Suicide bombing and shooting attack in Baghdad province, on the Shammari market area of Nahrawan. 11 dead, 35 wounded, 5 perps killed.

Dec 17, 2017: 1111, 12:22, 222, 4:44. 5:55

Dec 19, 2017 Event: Amtrak train derailment in Washington state. 3 killed, 100 injured.

Dec 26 & 27, 2017: 10:10, 11:11, 333, 444, 10:10, 12:12, 12.22, 1:11

Dec 28, 2017 Event: Apartment Blaze Bronx, 12 killed, including 5 children, 14 injured.

2018

Jan 19 & 20, 2018 11:11, 1212, 12:22, 10:10, 11:11, 1212.

Jan 23, 2018 Event: School Shooting, Kentucky. 2 dead, 18 injured

Feb 13, 2018 10:10, 11:11, 333, 444, 555, 10:10, 1212, 12:22, 1:11 2:22

Feb 14, 2018 Event: Mass shooting at Marjorie Stoneman Douglas High School, Parkland, Florida. 17 killed, 17 wounded, surpassing the Columbine high school massacre.

Notice that none of the sets of numbers were simply one pair, such as 11 or 22. They were all double-pairs, or triple numbers. While Judi's experiences with the phenomena of numbers are connected to such disturbing events, many of us experience number clusters related to relationships and events in our personal lives.

33, 3333

In August 2012, our daughter, Megan, was living in a high-rise apartment building in downtown Orlando with her dog, Nika, and a roommate. One evening, Megan took Nika down in the elevator for a walk outside and the door opened on a floor where a man with a leashed Pit Bull was waiting to get on. Without any provocation, the Pit Bull lunged at Nika and attacked her, its powerful jaws clamping down over her neck.

The fight that ensued left pools of blood everywhere. Nika had to undergo emergency surgery, had drainage tubes inserted in her neck for about ten days, all to the tune of about $1,300.

Within an hour of the attack, the Pit Bull's owner, Eric, was at the front desk, demanding to know who owned the black-and-white dog that had attacked his dog. The concierge informed him that the attack had been recorded by the security cameras and that *his* dog had attacked Megan's.

When Animal Care and Control showed up at Megan's apartment a couple of days after the attack, they asked if she wanted to cite the owner. The fine would be $200. Megan spoke to Eric, with Animal Care and Control on the line, and told him she wouldn't cite him if he agreed to pay the vet bill. He said he would.

A few days later, Megan presented Eric's girlfriend with copies of the vet bill. Megan said the young woman was very nice, was surprised the bill wasn't higher, and said that even though Eric said he would pay only half the bill—despite what he had told Megan—she had seen the video and would pay the other half. She promised Megan that she would have the money within a week, by Friday, August 18. Even though the Pit had been removed from the building by that date, Eric and his girlfriend still hadn't reimbursed Megan and he hadn't returned her calls, either.

Trish wrote a letter to Eric, telling him that if he hadn't reimbursed Megan by August 20, we would initiate legal action. She then headed down to Eric's apartment, knocked, rang the doorbell, but no one answered. So she taped the letter to the front door, unfolded, so anyone could read it.

Shortly before this, Megan and Trish had made a quick trip to the grocery store to pick up some things they needed. The bill came to $33.33. The only other time Trish had gotten repetitive numbers like this was in Costa Rica, with 111.11. She did a double take, immediately thought of Hexagram 33 in the *I Ching*, and her heart sank. That hexagram is called Retreat and she felt sure that Eric and his girlfriend had left town. What she didn't know was if they'd left town for the weekend, for a vacation, or for good.

Throughout the weekend in Orlando, we checked Eric's apartment several times to see if the note had been picked up. It was still taped to the front door of the apartment when we left that Sunday afternoon, August 19. The concierge at the front desk told Megan he hadn't seen Eric or his girlfriend for days.

Sure enough, Eric had blown town and Megan never was reimbursed for the vet bill.

This doesn't mean that if you repeatedly see 33 or 3333 that someone or something will retreat from your life or even that you'll be retreating. But because Trish uses the *I Ching* frequently, she associates 33 with the hexagram Retreat. You probably have other associations—a favorite radio station, for instance, or something fantastic that happened to you or someone you know at the age of 33, or maybe 33 was in the address of your childhood home. So if this is one of your repetitive numbers, play around with different definitions, see what resonates for you.

What about numbers that aren't repeats of each other? Can they exist in clusters, too? Yes. And some endure over the course of a lifetime.

#137 AND WOLFGANG PAULI

Wolfgang Pauli won the Nobel Prize in Physics in 1945 for his exclusion principle. He was an early supporter of Jung's theory on synchronicity and investigated the phenomenon as well. He had a rather striking experience with a set of numbers that lasted for most of his adult life.

Pauli was confounded by one of the unsolved mysteries of modern physics, the value of the fine structure constant, which involves the number 137. "The fine structure constant is one of those numbers at the very root of the universe and of all matter," writes Arthur I. Miller in *Deciphering the Cosmic Number: The Strange Friendship of Wolfgang Pauli and Carl Jung.* "If it were different, nothing would be as it is." As Miller explains in his fascinating book, 137 is not only the "DNA of light" but also the "sum of the Hebrew letters of the word 'Kabbalah.' The fine structure constant turns out to be exquisitely tuned to allow life as we know it to exist on our planet."

Heady stuff, and if it baffles physicists, the rest of us obviously don't have a clue. At best, most of us can understand that 137 is a prime number—a number that can only be divided by 1 and by itself. Or, put another way, a prime number is a positive integer that cannot equal the product of two smaller integers. But that's not what baffles physicists about 137. The number became so puzzling to physicists that the famed Richard Feynman, who won the Nobel Prize in Physics in 1965 for his contributions to the development of quantum electrodynamics, said that physicists should put a sign in their offices to remind themselves of how much they don't know. The sign would be simple: 137. Feynman called it "one of the greatest damn mysteries of physics: a magic number that comes to us with no understanding by man."

In 1934, Pauli began discussing his ideas publicly about 137 and Miller speculates that it might have been due to the effect of Jung's analysis "opening his mind to mystical speculation."

As physicist and author F. David Peat explained, "...while the other fundamental constants of nature are all immensely small or enormously large, this fine structure constant 1/137 turns out to be a human-sized number. This number...and its place in the scale of the universe particularly puzzled Pauli."

On December 5, 1958, Pauli was admitted to the hospital with agonizing stomach pains. When he learned he was in room 137, he told his assistant, Charles Enz, that he would never get out of the hospital alive. And he was right. During surgery, doctors discovered that Pauli had pancreatic cancer. He died in room 137 on December 15.

F. DAVID PEAT & #137

F. David Peat was a theoretical physicist who worked with the legendary physicist David Bohm in the 1970s and wrote *Synchronicity: The Bridge Between Matter and Mind*, one of the seminal books about synchronicity. In the later part of his life, he and his wife moved to Pari, Italy, where he started The Pari Center. Given his scientific background, his insights into synchronicity were unique.

We had a brief correspondence with him some years ago and he emailed this story about an experience he had with #137, when he was invited to give a lecture at the C. G. Jung Institute in Küsnacht, Switzerland, to celebrate the institute's fiftieth year.

"I arrived at the hotel next to the institute, was given a key and told my room was on the second floor of the annex. I didn't go to my room at once but went down to the lake. The idea was to get something of the spirit of Jung—but after half an hour, nothing happened at all. So I thought I'd go back to the hotel, sleep and maybe have a dream about Jung.

"I took the elevator to the second floor, removed the key

from my pocket and it was 137! And so I realized I was there to talk about Pauli and not Jung.

"That evening I told the story about the key and an old man at the back laughed. Later when I wrote an equation on the board, the same old man said, 'It won't work.'"

"I replied, 'Oh, the spirit of Pauli is in the room.'

"At the reception I asked who the old man was. It turned out that he was Charles Enz, the assistant who was with Pauli in the hospital," the one to whom Pauli remarked that he wouldn't get out of the hospital alive.

#137, TORONTO, & WEIRD OR WHAT?

In 2012, we were invited to appear on William Shatner's TV show, *Weird or What?* We were supposed to talk about a particular facet of Wolfgang Pauli's personality—something called The Pauli Effect—the spontaneous breakdown of laboratory equipment in his presence. This apparently telekinetic effect was to be presented as a possible theory for what was happening to a woman who believed she was the victim of government mind control.

We didn't know the specifics of the woman's story, but had collected quite a bit of information on the Pauli effect. As Miller explains in his book, "Physicists at the university (in Hamburg, Germany) became convinced that Pauli's presence in or even near a laboratory led to severe breakdowns in the equipment." Otto Stern, an experimental physicist who worked at the university, took desperate measures and forbade Pauli from entering the lab.

On a February weekend in 2012, we flew to Toronto. We were picked up at the airport on Friday evening by a service Shatner's production company provided. The car was spacious, comfortable, and gave us a chance to sit back and take in the city as the driver made his way through Friday rush hour traffic. At one point, the line of cars came to a complete standstill and Trish glanced out the window and couldn't believe what she saw.

There, on their right, was a building with prominent white

numbers on the front: 137, Pauli's number. And we were in town
to talk about Pauli.

Trish quickly nudged Rob and they both laughed. Then she
noticed that the building was a gym—Good Life Fitness—which
struck her as strangely ironic. 137 had proven to be Pauli's death
number, but we were here to talk about one facet of his *life*. The
synchronicity with #137 continued throughout the weekend.

On Sunday, we had some time before we were to be picked
up at our hotel, so we walked around downtown and found
ourselves on Yonge Street, where the gym was located. We
wanted to get a picture of the 137 and walked until we found it
and snapped some photos. We continued our walk and after a
few blocks one of us mentioned Pauli again. At that moment, we
both noticed a prominent sign across the street: WE'VE MOVED
to 137 YONGE. The building across from us apparently was the
former site of the gym.

When we returned to the hotel, we sat in the lobby and
Trish started emailing the photos to several friends whom she
knew would enjoy them. As she checked her iPad to make sure
the pictures were going through, she suddenly saw she had
emailed them at 1:37.

So Pauli greeted us as we entered Toronto, stuck around for
the weekend, and waved good-bye as we were waiting to leave.

PRACTICES: YOUR NUMBERS

Awareness. Maybe you've noticed certain numbers in
passing that pop up from time to time, but have never thought
much of it. Unless we're *aware* of the phenomenon of numbers,
the significance sails right past you. So without awareness,
number clusters aren't a placeholder in your life.

Exploration. Once you're aware of the numbers, though,
exploration is the next step, especially if the numbers appear
repeatedly. Your exploration, as you've seen in these anecdotes,
can take any number of paths and it doesn't matter how you
conduct your research as long as you find a meaning—your
vision—for the clusters that feels right to you, that fits your
situation.

Decipher the message. Figuring out what your number clusters mean can be tricky, as it was for Judi Hertling, or obviously, as it was for Pauli and Peat. Are the clusters confirmation? A warning? A hint of what's coming up?

On a computer file, list your most recent number clusters. What are the possible meanings of your clusters?

#18, WATERGATE, & THE TRUMP PRESIDENCY

History often provides us with stunning parallels to current events that involve numerical phenomenon.

In May 2017, Trump had been in office for about five months and the parallels between his administration's Russia scandals and those of the Nixon administration and Watergate already were becoming more apparent. One focal point was the number 18.

In Watergate, an 18-minute gap in a recording resulted in Nixon's impeachment and resignation. In the Russian investigation with this administration, it took Trump 18 days to fire National Security Advisor Michael Flynn after he was warned by acting Attorney General Sally Yates that Flynn might be easily blackmailed by the Russians.

On May 18, we learned from Reuters and the *New York Times* that there were at least 18 undisclosed contacts between members of the Trump administration and the Russians.

Hexagram 18 in the Richard Wilhelm edition of the *I Ching* is *Decay: work on what has been spoiled*. That message clearly resonates with the Flynn matter.

The repeating 18s underscored what many people were wondering. Was there a cover-up involved concerning the Trump campaign's link to the interference by Russia in our 2016 election? With this second set of 18s, we felt that the number might make even more appearances related to the Trump campaign. Then, in October of 2017, Paul Manafort, Trump's former campaign manager, was indicted on 18 counts of tax and bank fraud. On Aug. 21, Manafort was found guilty on eight of the 18 counts. A mistrial was declared on the other ten charges.

OTHER VENUES

The universe is endlessly creative, so it shouldn't come as any great surprise that numerical phenomenon manifest themselves in many ways, not just through our seeing numbers repetitively on clocks, receipts, microwaves. Events, situations, patterns can be repetitive, too.

In Jung's autobiography, *Memories, Dreams, Reflections*, co-authored with Angela Jaffe, he relates an interesting experience in which a fish motif turned up six times within a 24-hour period. On April 1, 1949, Jung made a note about an inscription that involved a fish. At lunch, he and his family had fish. During lunch, someone mentioned making an "April fish," a European term for "April fool."

That afternoon, a former patient he hadn't seen in months dropped by his home and showed him some paintings she'd done of fish. That evening, someone showed Jung a piece of embroidery with fish-like sea monsters on it. The next morning, another patient—one he hadn't seen for years—related a dream she'd had about fish.

At the time this cluster of synchronicities occurred, Jung was steeped in research on the symbolism of fish in Christianity, alchemy, and mythology. He noted that fish often represent unconscious contents. "This run of events made a considerable impression on me," Jung wrote. "It seemed to me to have a certain numinous quality."

This numinous quality is a characteristic many people mention when talking about their synchronicities, particularly those involving clusters. It's as if the hand of the cosmos sweeps into our lives and shakes things up so magically that we no longer see the world or ourselves in the same way.

To Jung, synchronicity was evidence of a unitary reality he called *unus mundus*, an alchemical expression that means one world. We were struck by this same sense of wonder in August 2009 when we experienced a cluster of 2s and 11s.

THE SWALLOWS

On August 19, 2009, we moved our daughter, Megan, back to college on Florida's west coast. On one stretch of highway there's nothing but sugar cane fields covering land that once was part of the Everglades. Along this stretch, hundreds of swallows sweep across the terrain in the early evening hours, nabbing insects on the fly, swooping across the two-lane road. They're especially thick around dusk and seem oblivious to cars.

On the way back to Florida's east coast, around dusk, we entered this stretch. The swallows swooped and dived (literally "sky-dived"), often winging away from our car at the last second. Then two of them, one after another, hit our windshield. At some deep level, we sensed it might be an omen. But of what?

On August 30, 11 days after we moved Megan back to college, we met her halfway across the state for her *second* skydive, for her 20th birthday. Her appointment was for 12:30, but they didn't get airborne until around 2 PM. She was jumping *tandem* with an instructor. We noticed the emerging pattern—second dive, 20th birthday, two swallows, a tandem jump at 2 PM.

The tandem jumpers left the plane last and there were just *two* of them. We were standing outside, watching the jumpers with four of Megan's friends. And suddenly, something happened to Megan's parachute. It seemed to just... well, fly away.

An instructor standing next to Trish exclaimed, "Wow, look at that."

"What just happened?" we asked.

"The first chute failed. Don't worry. They'll free-fall for a few seconds, then the *second* chute will open."

And that's exactly what happened. They landed safely and afterward Megan said she didn't even realize they'd lost the first chute. Later, another skydiver said it was an unusual occurrence. It didn't happen for him until his 1,200th dive.

Just look at the sequence of *11s* and *twos:* an event *11* days earlier that involved *two* diving swallows, was related to a *tandem* skydive that started at *2 PM* on our daughter's *20th* birthday, and it was the *second* chute that enabled them to land safely. Even though we knew the event with the swallows was symbolic of something, we didn't have any idea at the time what that something might be. But we were alert for patterns. That cluster proved to be precognitive.

Another facet of this synchronicity lies in the type of birds that flew into our windshield: swallows. These birds are known as *aerialists* because of their acrobatic twists and turns as they swoop after flying insects; a skydiver is a kind of aerialist, particularly during the free fall part of the dive. The incubation period for swallow eggs is from *11-20* days, more twos; *11* days after the swallows flew into our windshield, Megan went skydiving. Then there's the word swallow as a verb. It's as if the birds drew our attention to something we were supposed to swallow, to accept or understand.

"Our brains mathematically construct objective reality by interpreting frequencies that are ultimately projections from a deeper order of existence that is beyond space and time," wrote Michael Talbot in *The Holographic Universe.* "The brain is a hologram enfolded in a holographic universe."

PRACTICE: MORE NUMBERS

For a week, keep track of any number clusters you experience. As soon as you recognize a number cluster, jot down the circumstances when it began—how you were feeling, where you were, how the numbers appeared, and how many times. In the aftermath, take note of anything unusual that happened to you. Were the numbers connected in any way to that event?

10

ENCOUNTERS FROM BEYOND

"Watch the sky."
—Betty Hill

According to a *National Geographic* poll from 2012, almost 77% of Americans are sure that aliens have been on the Earth and 30% of Americans accuse the government of covering up the facts. The polls on the percentage of Americans who claim to have been abducted by aliens are all over the place—from a Roper poll that says the numbers are around four million to a Sci-fi/Roper UFO poll in 2002 that says one in seven Americans claim they or someone they know has had at least one "close encounter" of the "first, second, or third" kind. A first kind is seeing a UFO within 500 feet; a second is seeing evidence such as scorch mark or impressions from a landing; and a third is seeing beings inside or near the craft from a distance.

Whatever the true number, UFOs, aliens, and alien abductions remain beyond mainstream science and are officially dismissed by the U.S. government. However, a front-page story in the *New York Times* in December 2017 revealed that from 2007 to 2012, the Pentagon ran a program called the Advanced Aerospace Threat Identification Program. It was funded at the initiative of then Senate Majority Leader Harry Reid to investigate aerial threats, including what the military called "unidentified aerial phenomena" or just "objects." When the story was published, the Department of Defense claimed the program had ended in 2012.

But as Ralph Blumenthal, one of the authors of the story,

noted, "Our reporting suggested it continues, largely unfunded, to the present."

When it comes to encounters from elsewhere, truth is often elusive and convoluted. In spite of this, sightings and encounters reportedly continue.

A FAMOUS ENCOUNTER

The abduction of Betty and Barney Hill on September 19, 1961, is considered to be the beginning of what the late John E. Mack, former professor of psychiatry at Harvard Medical School, called "the modern history of abductions." It remains one of the most famous and controversial cases in ufology. In fact, if you Google "the Hill abduction," more than ten million hits come up. On YouTube, you can watch Betty recount her story about the abduction.

The Hill abduction established certain archetypal benchmarks of the experience: the sighting of unusual lights on a dark road—or in a dark room, missing time, loss of memory, a profound sense that something unusual and terrifying has occurred, or unusual marks on the body. When the Hills were hypnotically regressed separately to the night of the abduction, they both reported being taken aboard an E.T. craft, where experiments were performed on them. During their time on the craft, Betty allegedly saw a "star map" that she later was able to sketch.

Over the years and many subsequent books about their experience, the map is just one of many aspects of the story that skeptics have seized on as proof that their experience was delusional. We had an opportunity to question Betty Hill extensively about her experience one weekend in March 1986.

MEETING BETTY

In South Florida, March is usually a pleasant month. The scorching heat of summer hasn't arrived yet and mornings are still cool, with a gradual warming to the mid-seventies by afternoon. March 15, 1986, was that kind of day. The temperature was in the low sixties and traffic on I-95 flowed south beneath a vast panorama of cerulean blue sky. The tourist season would be in full swing until Easter, two weeks away, then the snowbirds would return north.

During the twenty-minute drive from our place in Fort Lauderdale to a UFO conference in Hollywood, we went over our list of questions for the featured speakers—Betty Hill and author and UFO investigator Budd Hopkins. The editor of *OMNI Magazine* was interested in articles on both of them.

At that time, *OMNI* was a unique entity among science magazines, a slick bimonthly launched by Kathy Keeton, the long-time companion and later the wife of *Penthouse* publisher Bob Guccione. In other words, it had plenty of financial backing. In the first issue, Guccione described the magazine as *"an original if not controversial mixture of science fact, fiction, fantasy and the paranormal."* It featured outstanding speculative and science fiction by writers who are now practically household names— Joyce Carol Oates, Orson Scott Card, William S. Burroughs, T. Coraghessan Boyle, even Stephen King. The magazine published an excerpt from King's *Firestarter.*

In the nonfiction area, they published articles on technology and cutting-edge ideas. One the most interesting pieces they published was on Robert Monroe, whose book, *Journeys Out of Body,* launched the Monroe Institute. Here, participants are guided through an exploration of consciousness, using techniques that Monroe developed. According to Monroe's stepdaughter, Nancy McMoneagle, now the director of the Monroe Institute, that *OMNI* piece put the institute on the map.

Our editor was interested in pieces for *OMNI's* Anti-Matter section, where articles about UFOs and the paranormal were featured. We were fledgling freelance writers who were delighted to get the assignment. Not only did it give us an opportunity to explore topics that interested us, but the magazine paid well and on time and we had the opportunity to meet fascinating people.

We had read *The Interrupted Journey,* John Fuller's account of the abduction of Betty and Barney Hill and had brought our copy along for her to autograph. We also had read Budd Hopkins' 1981 book *Missing Time*, the first book of its kind to map particular patterns of behavior among abductees. Missing time and screen memories were two such patterns.

Missing time, which the Hills experienced, usually involves the sighting of a light in the sky, then the abductee realizes that an hour or two or more have passed and the abductee can't recall what happened during that time. Sometimes the abductee is miles from where he or she last remembered being.

Screen memories sometime come into play when an abductee recalls seeing certain types of birds (owls are common) or animals (deer) or even small children in unusual places, like a bedroom. Or the abductee recalls a detailed sequence of events that have nothing to do with aliens or the abduction. In his book, Hopkins had some rather alarming speculations about cuts, scoops, and unexplained body scars that might be part of the abduction experience. He also maintained that some abductees had implants inserted into them, and may have experienced lifelong abductions.

The conference, sponsored by a New Age bookstore, wasn't well publicized and attracted less than a hundred people. The size made it easy for attendees and speakers to mingle comfortably.

Betty was the first speaker and she certainly didn't need notes for her talk. In her soft, gravelly voice, she described how on that cold September night in 1961, she and Barney were on their way home from a vacation in Canada. Betty, then a forty-one-year-old social worker and Barney, a thirty-nine-year-old postal worker, were driving along Route 3 through the White Mountains of New Hampshire to Portsmouth, where they lived. Around 10:15 PM, they noticed a bright light that moved erratically. They watched the light as they drove. Barney supposedly tried to convince himself that the light was an airplane, Betty thought it might be a communication satellite.

When they reached Indian Head, Barney stopped the car and got out for a closer look at the object through his binoculars. He saw lights of many colors and rows of windows on the object, which now moved toward him. When the object got to within a hundred feet of him, he could see occupants inside. Terrified, he ran back to the car where Betty waited and they sped away.

On their journey home, they heard a weird beeping sound in the car and suddenly realized they were thirty-five miles from where they had been moments ago. They arrived home at dawn, exhausted, and only later did they realize they couldn't account for at least two hours. A trip that should have taken them four hours had taken more than six.

In person, Betty was warm, funny, and hyper, constantly moving about and puffing on one cigarette after another. Her hands moved continually and sometimes trembled. She had a lot of nervous ticks in her facial expressions. She was sixty-seven then, Barney had been dead for seventeen years, and she had traveled to the conference with a close friend. She talked about her experience with passion and resolve, answered questions, and all the while, her pale blue eyes flicked from the crowd to the windows and back again.

After Betty's talk, we were sitting outside with her and her companion and scheduled a time for an interview for *OMNI* the next day. Budd Hopkins joined us as we were chatting with Betty and said he had been on a radio show that morning. One of the callers was a woman in Lake Worth, who claimed she had been abducted from her home the previous December. She had provided enough details to convince Hopkins that her story deserved further investigation. Since he hadn't rented a car, we offered to drive him to the woman's home.

DRIVING BUDD

During the forty-three-mile drive, Hopkins talked about some of the material that would be in his next book, *Intruders*—specifically the sexual experimentation many abductees reported that seemed to be related to reproduction. "In other words," Hopkins said, "these aliens are removing eggs from women and sperm from men. They're harvesting."

Some years later, David Jacobs, a Temple University historian who has hypnotically regressed more than a thousand abductees, many of them sent to him by Hopkins and other pioneers who were researching this phenomenon, expanded on Hopkins' findings. Jacobs identified urological and gynecological procedures that were performed on abductees, the presentation of infants and small children, and sexual activities, where abductees were forced to have sex with other abductees.

"Harvesting for what?" Rob asked. "And why?"

Hopkins shook his head. "Who knows? For crossbreeding? To create a race of hybrids?"

Eight years after this drive with Hopkins, John Mack, professor of psychiatry at Harvard, published *Abduction: Human Encounters with Aliens*, one of the most comprehensive books about the phenomenon. He described these procedures that Hopkins mentioned where "instruments are used to penetrate virtually every part of the abductees' bodies." In addition to removing sperm from men and eggs from women, "abductees experience being impregnated by the alien beings and later having an alien-human or human-human pregnancy removed." During subsequent abductions, the abductees may see incubators where the hybrid babies are living or may be asked to hold the babies.

Intuitively, Budd Hopkins knew he was onto something, that he had recognized vitally important patterns in the abduction phenomenon, and he felt the woman who had called into the radio show might reveal additional pieces of that pattern under hypnosis. He also mentioned that he'd been working with a famous author whose abduction experiences spanned many years. "He's writing his book now. And I'm telling you, when this book is published, it will be explosive."

We pressed him for the name of the writer, but Hopkins wouldn't tell us. We figured it out less than a year later, when in February 1987, William Morrow published Whitley Strieber's *Communion*. It was a harrowing account of the writer's abduction experiences that spanned more than a decade. In the book, he described the experiments that were performed on him, many of them dovetailing with what Hopkins had found.

Since Strieber was already a popular and successful writer of fiction, including *The Hunger* and *The Wolfen*, he was accused of writing fiction as though it were fact, was ridiculed for his description of rectal probes, was reviled by skeptics, and the book, which hit the *New York Times* bestseller list, got mixed reviews. His fiction career suffered. He eventually lost his home in upstate New York where the abductions had occurred.

But Strieber persevered, continued to write fiction and nonfiction, and in 2019, has one of the most comprehensive websites about the abduction scenario, E.T.s, alternate realities, and mysteries of the unknown. His podcast, *Dreamland*, features researchers, abductees, writers, and offers fascinating insights into the matrix of reality in which we live.

On this early afternoon in March of 1986, though, all of that lay in the future. We were just three people on our way to a Lake Worth home where a woman claimed to have been abducted by aliens. Somewhere en route Budd suddenly became suspicious about how we had appeared right when he needed a ride and were willing to take him on an hour-long drive. He asked us about our backgrounds and suggested that freelance writers could be a good cover for government agents. Apparently, he thought a federal agency might be monitoring his activities. Rob told him that such agents would probably be driving a new rental vehicle and that our ten-year-old Mazda with its faulty air conditioner didn't fit that profile. That seemed to satisfy him.

HOPKINS REGRESSES AN ABDUCTEE

Since its incorporation in 1911, the city of Lake Worth has covered less than seven square miles in Palm Beach County. As of 2016, the town has nearly 38,000 residents, including one of the largest Finnish communities in America. Artists have discovered beauty in its old downtown buildings and neighborhoods. But back in 1986, it was a sleepy place inhabited mostly by retirees. Its one distinction was that Lake Worth was the home office of the *National Enquirer,* which was located several blocks from our destination.

Upon arriving, Cathy and Jake Bristol welcomed us to their modest-sized home in a middle-class neighborhood. Cathy seemed nervous, but anxious to tell us her story and eager to

see if Budd could regress her back to her abduction. Budd had
selected her from among the callers because she had become
upset by what Budd was saying in the radio interview, and was
convinced that she was an abductee. She knew something had
happened to her one night when three child-sized beings had
appeared in her bedroom and floated her away.

While Budd prepared Cathy for the regression, Rob talked to
Jake, who was five or six years older than his wife. He was in his
early forties and sported a mane of silver hair that flowed over
his collar and a matching full beard. He was dressed completely
in black. His shirt was partially open and he wore a necklace
with a gold devil head dangling from it. He bluntly told Rob
that he was a former Baptist minister, who had switched sides.
Did his presence have anything to do with Cathy's experience?
Did his petitions to Satan attract the three Grays, who would
abduct his wife?

Interestingly, Budd ignored Jake. He hardly seemed to notice
him. He was fully focused on Cathy. If he noticed the satanic
emblem hanging from Jake's neck, he didn't inquire about it or
take any interest in Jake's role in Cathy's experience.

Cathy related all that she remembered before Hopkins
hypnotized her. She had awakened during the night to find
three small beings at the foot of her bed. They resembled little
kids. She wondered how they had gotten into her bedroom
and why they were just standing there. They didn't speak,
didn't move. Then suddenly she was paralyzed, still breathing
but unable to move even her little finger. Yet, her mind was
functioning—shocked, incredulous, but aware—and she knew
something terribly disturbing, frightening beyond words, was
happening to her.

Cathy recalled being floated from her bed by these three
small beings with large heads. As this was happening, her
husband remained motionless on the bed, in a sleep-like death.
They moved her down the hall, through a wall—as if it were
a doorway—and out into the back yard. A transparent tube
appeared that transported her into the starlit sky toward a
hovering craft. While rising in the tube, she looked down at a
huge Christmas tree displayed on the property of the *National*

Enquirer, a rather ironic twist because at the time, the tabloid was famous for publishing UFO stories.

The tree was fully lit and Carol pointed it out to the aliens. Hopkins matter-of-factly asked how they reacted, and Cathy, speaking in a soft monotone replied, "They don't react. They aren't impressed." (Our editor at *OMNI* loved that part of the story.)

The Christmas tree was the last familiar thing she consciously remembered before disappearing into the vessel.

Under hypnosis, she described being placed on a table. Her clothes were gone, she didn't remember removing them. A taller entity hovered over her, studying her, its head close to hers, its black eyes peering into hers. She felt it was invading her mind, her soul. She thought of her ten-year-old son asleep in the house and wondered if she would ever see him again.

The tall entity held a metallic instrument in its hand and forced it into her nose and sinuses. She tried to scream, but couldn't move, couldn't make a sound. The entity spoke to her, its lips not moving, and told her to stop struggling, that it would be over soon. He stepped to the other end of the table and Carol felt a cold instrument penetrating her genitals, moving deep inside her. She didn't know how long the procedure lasted, and had no memory of leaving the craft.

When she awakened in the morning, she was in her own bed. She felt bruised, abused, profoundly depressed, and didn't know why. Cathy, like Betty Hill, didn't remember what had happened to her until the memories began to return to her first in dreams. Then she heard Budd Hopkins on the radio, describing alien abductions, and she became extremely nervous and uneasy. She knew without a doubt that something eerily similar had happened to her. She called the radio station and talked to Hopkins on the air. In recalling bits and pieces of her experience, she had a difficult time controlling her emotions.

Before leaving, we walked out into the Bristols' small back yard where Cathy had said the tube had first appeared. Hopkins looked around, gazed up at the night sky. "Yeah, there would be enough room back here," he said.

During the regression, Cathy's husband, Jake, had watched

closely, occasionally fingering the devil head around his neck. Jake was an imposing figure and we kept exchanging glances, wondering what was up with him. We later puzzled over Cathy's situation. She seemed dominated in her daily life by her peculiar husband. Then little Grays abducted her, controlled her, and abused her. We couldn't help but wonder if the abduction scenario had been a psychological event, a metaphor for her life. Yet, Hopkins was convinced that the event had taken place in the physical world. We listened to the tape of the compelling regression we had witnessed, and decided that maybe it was both.

Hopkins stayed overnight with the Bristols and took a taxi to the airport the next day. For our part, we were eager to leave the house. After several hours listening to and discussing Cathy's eerie tale combined with her husband's formidable presence, we were relieved to be on our way.

Earlier at the conference, Hopkins had dismissed the idea that he might be an abductee himself. Out there in the Bristols' yard, Rob asked, "Budd, do you think your work with abductees has affected your art?"

He stood there, quiet a moment, then said, "I hope not."

In spite of his comment, we had the sense that Hopkins had long since realized that his life as a respected Manhattan artist was taking second place to his life as an author and abduction investigator. In his memoir, *Art, Life and UFOs*, published in 200, he talks about this dichotomy in his life. He also notes that someone had asked him if he believed UFOs really existed and if the thousands of accounts by abductees were actually true. "I recall answering, sadly, I no longer had the luxury of *dis*belief. Even back in the 1970s I felt the sense of being helpless in the face of the accumulating evidence, and aware that the UFO phenomenon made the future seem increasingly ominous."

He went on to establish the Intruders Foundation, continued to regress abductees, and to collect information that resulted in several other books. The following year, his book *Intruders* was published and became a *New York Times* bestseller.

AN EVENING WITH BETTY HILL

We returned to the conference the next day for an interview with Betty. We invited Betty and her friend to our townhouse in Fort Lauderdale, and they agreed to join us that evening. We were somewhat embarrassed when we entered the place, what with dust bunnies hiding under the TV and stereo, and books and files cluttering tabletops and spilling onto the floor. But neither Betty nor her friend seemed to notice.

We put together a platter of veggies, cheese, and fruit, brought out some beer, and sat in the living room, where Betty entertained us with stories about all the UFO sightings she'd seen since she and Barney were abducted. Once Betty was talking, there was no interrupting her. She was in the flow, out there, *gone.*

She was an affable woman with a quick laugh and a terrific sense of humor. But when she started talking about what had happened to her and Barney, the mirth bled away. Her eyes seemed haunted, particularly as she described the details. There were eleven Grays. She referred to one of them as the leader, because he seemed to be in charge and was the only one who "spoke English." Then there was the examiner, the Gray who conducted the physical tests, and nine other crew members.

She and Barney were examined in separate rooms. Under hypnosis several years after their experience, they both reported that the examiner took samples of their hair, fingernails, and skin, examined their eyes, nose, throat, and ears, and tested their nervous systems. When the examiner brought out an instrument with a long needle and Betty was told he was going to insert it into her navel, she was beyond terrified. "I wanted to know what they were about to do to me. The leader explained it was a pregnancy test. I told him it would hurt..." But the examiner inserted the needle despite her protests and she squirmed in agony until the leader touched Betty's forehead and the pain went away.

Under hypnosis, Barney recalled that sperm was taken from him.

At one point, Betty seemed overwhelmed by her memories and abruptly pushed her chair back from the table, stood, and headed for the sliding glass doors, opened them, and vanished outside. The rest of us hurried after her and found Betty in the middle of the parking lot in front of our townhouse, arm moving slowly, finger pointed skyward, following a light. "See that?" she exclaimed. "See that light?"

We glanced at each other, both of us thinking the same thing. The light came from a plane. But it was Betty's friend who voiced the obvious.

"No," Betty responded with a shake of her head. "They can camouflage themselves. They're masters of camouflage."

Well, maybe they are, who can say for sure? But the point wasn't the light—plane, satellite, UFO—it was that she uttered this statement with the same resolve we had noticed during her passionate talk at the conference.

"When Barney and I…what we experienced, what we saw… what happened…" She talked in fits and starts, as if she couldn't spit the words out quickly enough.

And suddenly, standing out there in the parking lot beneath a sky strewn with stars, any doubts we had about Betty Hill vanished. Utterly. Completely. This woman and her husband had experienced *something* out there on Route 3, on September 19, 1961. But *what?*

Whatever it was, the event sculpted the rest of Betty's life. Because of Fuller's book, a subsequent article in *Look* Magazine, and then a movie, she and Barney became internationally known as the first modern-day UFO abductees. Rather than hiding her experience, Betty spoke out and expressed the collective experience of those who came later.

The procedure Betty described—the needle through her navel—sounds similar to amniocentesis. During an amniocentesis, a small amount of fluid is taken from the amniotic sac surrounding a developing fetus and the fetal DNA is examined for genetic abnormalities. The gender of the fetus can also be determined. But this procedure wasn't known in 1961 and didn't come into widespread use until the late 1980s.

Both Betty and Barney suffered from nightmares and

profound anxiety in the aftermath of their experience. In late 1963, they underwent hypnotic regression with Benjamin Simon, a physician in Boston. During one session, Dr. Simon gave Betty a post-hypnotic suggestion that she could sketch a copy of the three-dimensional "star map" she had seen on the ship. She eventually did so and drew twelve prominent stars that stood out in her memory, with three smaller, dimmer stars. The stars were connected by lines and dashes. The solid lines, Betty said, were trade routes. The dashes represented routes to less-traveled stars.

In 1968, an elementary school teacher and amateur astronomer, Marjorie Fish, decided to decipher Betty's star map to see if it was possible to determine the star system from which the UFO originated. She constructed a three-dimensional model of nearby Sun-like stars using thread and beads. It wasn't until 1969, when the update to the *Gliese Star Catalogue*, titled the *Catalogue of Nearby Stars*, was published, that she was able to make a determination.

The Gliese is a modern star catalogue of stars located within twenty-five parsecs of Earth. One parsec is roughly three-point-two-six light years or about nineteen trillion miles. Fish, after studying thousands of vantage points, decided the one that seemed to be the best match was from a double star system, Zeta Reticuli. Fish concluded that the UFO that abducted the Hills may have originated from a planet orbiting Zeta Reticuli.

Most scientists, Carl Sagan among them, dismissed the map. But Walter Mitchell, an astronomer and professor at Ohio State University, believed Fish's calculations were correct. In the December 1974 issue of *Astronomy Magazine*, he said: "The pattern discovered by Marjorie Fish has an uncanny resemblance to the map drawn by Betty Hill. The stars are mostly ones that we would visit if we were exploring from Zeta Reticuli. The travel patterns make sense."

SECOND VISIT WITH THE ABDUCTEE

We were curious about how the Bristols—Cathy in particular—fared in the months after her regression. We had spoken to them by phone several times and we finally invited them to our place for dinner. We should have guessed that doing so would attract more high strangeness.

We decided to make it a small dinner party with a few others who were interested in the abduction scenario. Among them were Renie Wiley, a psychic and empath who worked with local police on the well-known Adam Walsh case, and psychic Tony Grosso, with whom Rob later co-authored *The Rainbow Oracle*, a book of color divination. Only Renie had experienced UFO encounters.

Cathy and her husband arrived early. Once again, Jake wore black and that gold satanic symbol around his neck. Jake was strangely quiet that night, and seemed out of his element, wary of everyone. He never moved from his chair—not to stretch, not to use the bathroom. Cathy talked a little about her abduction, but mostly we just sat around talking and having a good time. Except for Jake.

Around 1 AM, while we were talking about men in black (MIBs)—not the Tommy Lee Jones movies, which didn't come out until years later—the unexpected happened. Rob glanced over at the sliding glass doors leading from the living room to a small porch and the parking lot. There, on the porch, peering in at us, was a man dressed in black. By the time Rob alerted everyone else, the man had moved away.

Rob ran to the doors, slid them open, and could hardly believe what he saw. The man, instead of simply disappearing into the darkness beyond the parking lot, was making a scene of his escape. Crouching low, he darted from car to car like a cat, and kept glancing back at us, hiding in full view.

Trish called the police and the response astounded us. Within a few minutes, five or six patrol cars arrived, sirens shrieking, and cops with dogs spread out across the complex, searching for the man. What? We were baffled by the response to the relatively minor incident until we were told that someone had been murdered an hour earlier, less than a mile away, and the killer was on the loose.

As far as we know, they never found the man *we* reported, and we don't know if he had anything to do with the murder. But it was a strange ending for an unusual evening, and we never saw the Bristols again.

The next day, Renie called to tell us what she thought of the Bristols. She believed that Cathy's story was legit. They had apparently talked at one point in the kitchen, away from the rest of us. Renie also suspected that Jake's involvement in the "dark arts" may have attracted these negative entities.

We knew what Renie meant. But is it that simple?

WHITLEY STRIEBER

In February 1987, we walked into a Waldenbooks in a mall in Fort Lauderdale. There, on the new releases display, was a book that featured the face of an alien Gray, with its huge, dark, almond-shaped eyes, tiny mouth, and slits for nostrils. That face is now well-known, but back then, it was new and frightening. Over the years since reading *Communion*, we followed Strieber's career with great interest. But it wasn't until 2010, when Trish published a novel with TOR, also Strieber's publisher, that we became acquainted.

Trish's editor approached Strieber about endorsing her novel, *Esperanza*, and after that, they exchanged emails periodically. In 2011, our book *The 7 Secrets of Synchronicity* was published and Strieber invited us to talk with him on his podcast, *Dreamland*. It was the first of many appearances. We got to know him and his wife, Anne, and Strieber was always generous with his time and invitations.

In early January 2018, Strieber emailed us saying that he'd been told to go to Cassadaga, Florida. Did we know about the spiritualist village, and was there any chance that we could meet him there? Synchronistically, the email arrived just as we were leaving Cassadaga, where Trish had taught an astrology workshop. The timing of the email caught our attention. We agreed on a date and on January 23, we met him and author and researcher Peter Levenda in the town where everyone talks to the dead.

Levanda, an author of numerous books on the occult, had just published his latest tome, *Sekret Machines: Gods: Volume 1 of Gods, Man & War*, co-authored with Tom Delonge, an unusual look at UFOs that cleverly blends the phenomenon with occult history.

Over dinner, Strieber talked about how he has been in contact with his deceased wife, Anne, since her passing in 2015, and how they had co-authored a book, *The Afterlife Revolution*. Levenda talked about his work with Tom Delonge related to UFOs and encounters.

One of the most fascinating points in the discussion involved Strieber's implant, which he said was inserted against his will by two humans—not aliens. He explained how it affects the vision in his left eye. It's as if a slit opens in his vision and words scroll across it. He has to adjust where he looks to be able to decipher it. The implant was inserted behind his left ear when he and Anne were living in their cabin in upstate New York, where his earliest abduction experiences took place. He told us that when he had surgery to remove the implant, it moved and he decided it was best to leave it in place.

One of the most interesting facets of these conversations was Strieber's contention that abductions are no longer happening with the frequency they were in the 1980s and 1990s and through the early part of the twenty-first century. "They have what they need from us," he said.

"Which is what?" we asked.

Strieber shrugged. "DNA, knowledge about who we are, our psyches."

At the core of all of these conversations lay questions about the nature of reality, how paranormal experiences—and contact with aliens (or whatever they are) and spirits—alter how you see the world and yourself within it. For most of the evening and the next day, we felt like we were in the company of ancient alchemists.

Strieber told us he still has frequent contact with the entities he calls visitors. He also continues to explore the nature of the afterlife through his interactions with his wife and through the visitors. Early on in his experiences, he discovered that encounters often included the dead—deceased relatives or loved ones who were with the visitors. This phenomenon has been reported by other abductees and people who've experienced encounters.

During that time we spent in Cassadaga, we speculated about why this is a motif in some encounters. It may be that the visitors—aliens, our future selves, entities from another dimension, whatever they are—and the dead inhabit the same time/space. Alternately, perhaps the visitors believe that we'll be comforted by the presence of dead loved ones and cloak themselves in the images they pull from our minds. Then again, it may be something else altogether. We just *don't know.* And that quest for answers, for understanding the nature of the visitors, is what drives speculation and curiosity.

A CLASSIC ABDUCTION

The night of November 9, 1981 was cold and clear in southern Georgia. The sky was cloudless, lit up by stars, and thirty-eight-year old Connie J Cannon, an R.N., was excited.

She, her husband, and their three sons were relocating from their home outside of Atlanta to St. Augustine Beach, Florida. She was driving a brand-new Regency Oldsmobile sedan with a V8, 454-cubic inch engine, a large, powerful automobile that was a dream to drive, especially on I-75. The rear seat and trunk were loaded with boxes of belongings. Her youngest son, John, twelve, was in the passenger seat and they were following a huge moving van driven by her husband, Ted, who was accompanied by her other two sons. They were about a hundred miles south of Atlanta, near Macon, traffic was negligible, when she suddenly realized she was no longer on the interstate.

Connie was certain she hadn't taken an exit. Yet, she and her son were now driving on a strange grid of roads with no buildings in sight. She didn't see anything she recognized. She was incredibly tired, but kept driving. The next thing she knew, she and her son were on their knees outside their vehicle, on a black asphalt tarmac near airplane hangars, and were sobbing hysterically.

Circling overhead were several noisy helicopters and three round, softly grumbling circular spacecraft. In front of her and John were a group of Grays and several military men wearing fatigues and heavy boots who held assault weapons.

The Grays seemed to be just loitering in the area, but one of the military men pointed his weapon directly at Connie, and in a menacing tone, warned her, "If you ever...you will never see your family again."

Ever *what*? What was it she wasn't supposed to do or say? Why would the military be concerned about what she might or might not do or say? Why were aliens mingling with the military? What the hell was going on?

Then she and John found themselves back in the car and she had no memory of actually getting into the vehicle. Where were the military men? The Grays? The choppers and spacecraft? What kind of vision was that?

Her son immediately fell into a deep sleep. Connie, barely able to keep her eyes open, recalls driving aimlessly around a labyrinth of paved roads, clueless about where she was. No houses. No landmarks. Just another grid of streets. She finally saw a convenience store and stumbled inside. She tried her best to sound coherent as she told the female clerk that she'd gotten lost off of I-75, and could she please give her directions back to the interstate.

The clerk told Connie she was on Warner Robins Air Force Base and had to leave through the same guard gate where she'd entered. Connie explained she hadn't come through a guard gate, but the clerk insisted she couldn't have gotten onto the base any other way. Connie realized that arguing with the woman was futile and besides, she was so exhausted she could hardly speak. "Just point me in the right direction," Connie said.

She followed the clerk's instructions and eventually found her way back to I-75.

By that time, her husband and other two sons were frantic with worry. When Ted realized that the Olds was no longer behind him, he pulled off the road to wait, thinking they had just dropped back. When they didn't appear after a few minutes, Ted took the next exit and drove northward for a while to see if he spotted the Olds by the side of the road. In 1981, there were no cell phones, no way to make contact. He finally figured that Connie and John must have gotten off the interstate for a pit stop or to get a bite to eat, and he and their other sons headed south again.

But, once more, Ted pulled to the shoulder of the road to wait for his wife and son. When the Olds didn't appear, the only thing Ted and the other two boys could do was head toward their new home and hope that Connie and John would catch up to them. They arrived at their new house and waited. An hour passed, then another, and Connie and John still didn't show. Ted, completely panicked, was on the verge of calling the highway patrol when Connie and John finally pulled into the driveway. They'd been missing for three hours.

Connie was too exhausted and confused to explain to Ted what had happened. She and John fell into a deep sleep on the porch of their new home and were disoriented for several days afterward. It was worse than jet lag, more like post-traumatic stress syndrome. "Traumatic doesn't begin to describe the incident," Connie says. "Staring into the barrel of an assault rifle held by one of our own military personnel, while three Grays looked on, was beyond my cognitive abilities."

She's thankful that her young son was spared that memory. He only recalled being lost and driving on a grid of streets with no buildings nearby. "He doesn't recall the incident, but he does know something awful happened, and he *does* know that since that incident, the 'visitors' have intruded into his home at night."

ABDUCTED ON A MILITARY BASE?

Warner Robins Air Force Base is located just east of and adjacent to the city of Warner Robins, Georgia, eighteen miles SSE of Macon, Georgia. Today, the town of Warner Robins has a population of around 63,000. Macon, the state's fourth largest city, lies a short distance to the north. I-16 intersects with I-75 in Macon and leads to Savannah and the Atlantic Ocean. According to the base's website, Warner Robins AFB "is the worldwide manager for a wide range of aircraft, engines, missiles, software and avionics and accessories components."

Even today, there are long, lonely stretches of I-75 from around Macon to Valdosta and at night, it's easy to become disoriented. Looming to your right and left are places your headlights don't penetrate, places bogeymen might hide. You can almost see some alien craft hovering silently, touching down. The imagination is a trickster. Anything is possible.

Yet, Connie is certain she didn't turn off the interstate. So how did she end up wandering around a "grid of streets" on an Air Force base fifteen to eighteen miles from the interstate? How did she get onto the base? The only way to access the base was through guard gates secured by armed military police, and you needed a pass to get in. So how did that heavy Olds, packed with belongings, a woman and a kid, get onto the tarmac? And, even following the clerk's direction, how did Connie get *off* the base if the only way off was through a security gate?

When you step back from Connie's memories, you have to ask what a convenience store is doing on a military base. Yes, there are commissaries. But a commissary is quite different from your local 7-Eleven that sells gas, beer and wine, cigarettes and lottery tickets. Several years after we wrote about Connie's experience, a friend who lives in the area reported that there actually is a 7-Eleven on the base.

But for Connie, that doesn't answer the bottom line questions: Were the military officers actually Grays, who had shape-shifted, a ruse created by the aliens to confuse and distract from what was actually happening? Were they even *on* a military base? Were they somehow transported by alien technology?

Connie doesn't know. But she is convinced she was abducted and that it was one of many alien abductions she has experienced since the age of four.

We met Connie in 2003 after she read Trish's novel, *Black Water*, and wrote a fan letter. The story features a bookstore owner whose daughter is kidnapped and taken back in time by a sociopathic time traveler. For the next few years, they exchanged emails, then in 2005 Trish had a psychic reading with Connie. Much of what she predicted unfolded. They stayed in touch.

In February 2009, we started a blog on synchronicity and Connie was one of the first who commented. In October 2010, we posted a story called *The Abduction* about her experience on

Warner Robins Air Force Base, the first time she had publicly told the story. That post drew more than a hundred comments, including some from ardent skeptics who thought she was either lying or mentally unstable.

While studies show that abductees tend to be as mentally stable as the general population, they are profoundly traumatized by their experiences. As we've mentioned before, they often have memory loss and unexplained physical scars— punctures or incision marks in their skin, scrapes or burns. And sometimes they have unexplained nosebleeds.

One of Connie's most unusual encounters occurred some years later, in St. Augustine, around 3 AM. She awakened to find herself standing in her nightgown, on a street corner a couple of blocks from her home. She became aware of a rumbling sensation under her feet and knew what it meant.

Three space vehicles were approaching and she knew the ships held beings that would control her, leave her ill, listless, and despairing. Her abject terror prompted her to hide somewhere, anywhere, in the shadows, under trees. She desperately tried to camouflage herself, to make herself small, like an ant, or a blade of grass. But to no avail.

A single craft separated from the other two and suddenly she was inside that vessel, seated in what looked like a desk chair. A metal strap automatically stretched across her belly, restraining her. She didn't have any idea how she had gotten from the street to the craft.

Connie felt the ship moving and spinning at the same time, and when it abruptly stopped, it quivered like a leaf in the wind. She thought she might vomit. An entity loomed in front of her, one of the Grays with large black eyes, a negligible nose, a tiny lipless mouth, and sallow gray skin. He spoke in a metallic voice, a monotone, and ordered her to look down.

She did so and a large shield slid open under her seat, revealing a transparent floor, "like a glass-bottom boat at Silver Springs, Florida." A light came on and she could see a house below the craft, and somehow the light penetrated the roof and revealed the interior of the house—the various rooms and furniture, even people sleeping in their beds.

She wasn't afraid; she was enraged. She demanded, "*What? What do you want me to see? These people are asleep. It's the middle of the night. What do you want me to see?*"

All the while, the gray entity was right in front of her, staring into her eyes. That made her even more furious.

Then, just like that, it was morning and she was back in bed.

She sat up, her nightgown soiled with grass stains and dirt, and suddenly, blood poured from her right nostril. The right side of her body felt numb. The room spun when she stood. She thought she might have had a stroke and shouted for her husband. By the time they reached the hospital, Connie couldn't walk. Ted had to carry her into the emergency room.

A CAT scan revealed that her brain was not bleeding. There were no blood clots, no aneurysm, no stroke. Nothing unusual was found, except for a small anomalous shadow that appeared on the right side of her nose in a sinus scan, what she later believed was an implant. She went home without explaining anything to Ted or anyone else about her experience. Yet, she knew it had happened. That it was *real.*

Connie describes herself as a "reasonable, rational, moderately intelligent woman who finds a tremendous degree of joy in her life. I don't think I'm prone to hysterics or exaggerations. I've been a hands-on caregiver for the terminally ill, and have worked in medical research and in a technical medical teaching capacity. I'm grounded and fact-oriented."

At the same time, she admits that in the aftermath of an encounter with the Grays, her challenge is always to remain sane and not to live her life in utter terror.

LONG-TERM SYMPTOMS

Many long-time abductees experience symptoms that include phobias and various health problems that span decades. Diana Fine used to suffer from such severe nosebleeds as a child that when she was nine, her parents had her sinuses cauterized. Connie has ended up in the emergency room a number of times for unexplained bleeding. Jennifer White grew up with a lot of "night fears" and is still uneasy about "shadows." She suffers from periodic migraines that lay her up for days.

An abductee we knew years ago was so traumatized by his experience that his life unraveled at the seams. Don Estrella, whose last name ironically means star in Spanish, retained partial memories of an alien abduction that occurred while he was en route to a costume party.

When we met him in the mid-1980s, he was essentially a lost and homeless person, but with an intriguing and colorful background. He had worked as an assistant to author John Keel at the time Keel was delving into the chilling Mothman saga in West Virginia, which later became a book, *The Mothman Prophecies*, and in 2002 a movie with the same title starring Richard Gere. Estrella reveled in telling stories related to the giant red-eyed flying beast. He had also worked in a clerical position at the United Nations, where he started a UFO club. He recalled that then-UN Secretary General U Thant sent someone from his office to attend the initial meeting.

Curious about his abduction experience, we persuaded Estrella to undergo a hypnotic regression with psychiatrist Dr. Berthold Schwarz of Vero Beach, Florida. The author of *UFO Dynamics*, Schwarz had interviewed or regressed hundreds of contactees or "UFO observers," as he often called them.

In an article for *Medical Times*, Schwarz wrote that these contactees were not psychotic or suffering from hallucinations and they weren't publicity-seekers. "More, on the contrary, fearing ridicule, they are embarrassed to testify to what they saw."

During the session, Estrella recalled a bizarre scene in which he was abducted on a North Virginia highway on Halloween night, while he was wearing a pirate's costume and his companion was dressed as a clown.

They never made it to the Halloween party. The engine in their car died and wouldn't start. That's when three small beings appeared and escorted them to a waiting circular craft. They joined seven or eight other abductees standing in line in an obvious stupor.

Estrella sobbed throughout the regression as he described

being taken aboard, placed naked on a table, examined and probed. While those procedures are now common descriptions by abductees, Estrella also recalled seeing strange symbols on the interior wall of the craft. During hypnosis, he drew several of the alien symbols.

While Estrella was haunted for more than two decades by his experience and seemed lost because of it, Mack pointed out that some abductees have experienced physical healings and spiritual transformations as a result of their abductions. Estrella apparently developed psychic abilities in the aftermath of his experience and, as we recall, was happiest sitting in a restaurant with a cup of coffee and a cigarette and giving free readings to the waitresses. He was fairly talented at tuning into near-future events and reading a person's past.

In 1991, Diane Fine worked on the waterfront at a marina and had to climb numerous stairs each day. Her left knee throbbed constantly. Even though she was a military wife at the time, she hadn't had a chance to go to the clinic. One night, she woke and found herself on a familiar surgical table. A big light shone overhead, but she could still see the Grays. Four of them were gathered at her feet—three small entities and one tall one. The larger one always seemed to be in charge and this time was no exception. She realized they had operated on her knee, that they could do that, so she asked them, "Why don't you fix my autoimmune disorder?"

"We can't. It's karmic. This (the knee) is mechanical."

Then Debra lost consciousness. "The next morning, I checked my knee. There was a small incision. It healed within two days. My knee has never bothered me again."

Individuals who undergo spiritual transformation as a result of their experiences, Mack said, are more "open to other realities beyond space/time…" And some abductees experience numerous synchronicities or meaningful coincidences that seem to act as guidance, confirmation, and support.

It seems that merely coming into contact with abductees can result in synchronicity. While we were working on Connie's story about her experience on Warner Robins Air Force base, we happened to check Statcounter on our synchronicity blog, which provides all kinds of statistics about the people who visit. We were astonished to see that someone from Warner Robins, Georgia, had arrived at our blog by Googling the phrase: *Warner Robins military secrets.* In the more than three years we'd had the blog, we had never noticed a hit from Warner Robins, Georgia. What are the odds that someone dropped by, using those search words, just as we were writing Connie's story?

THE MAKING OF AN ABDUCTEE

John Mack noted in *Abduction* that efforts to characterize abductees as a group haven't been successful. "They seem to come, as if at random, from all parts of society." And even now, two decades after the publication of his book, that statement apparently still holds true.

We asked Diane Fine, a lifelong abductee mentioned earlier, why she thought she had been taken. "It seems to me that some humans are *marked* and the answer is part of a larger view that encompasses something bigger than one lifetime. I now view these abduction experiences as just one form of my lifetime of psychic experiences. I have also seen other types of beings. Some angelic, some demonic and a wide range in between. It also seems that being human is something the Grays don't get to do, and they desperately want to "grok" us. They are obsessed with why we are attracted to other beings: mates, pets, children, even rock idols. Our nature to feel desire seems to interest them."

A WILLING PARTICIPANT

Diane's comment about being "marked" is echoed by another lifelong abductee, Susan Yantorno. A retired veterinarian, she is willing to tell her story so others will know that not all so-called abductees find their interactions with aliens terrifying. Susan is a willing participant in experiences that have been going on for decades.

Her first contact with the "beings," as she prefers to call them, occurred when she was seven or eight years old during a summer that she spent at her grandparent's farm. It was night and she was standing in the front field in her flannel nightgown down by the creek near the apple orchard. There were five beings nearby and they were about her size. She didn't feel frightened or threatened. She thought of them as friends. That was all she can recall from that encounter, which came to mind in a self-hypnosis session when she posed the question about her first contact. In the years that followed, there were more contacts.

Since the late 1990s, she has experienced frequent contact with both physical and spirit beings. Susan's contact is considerably different from the textbook alien abductee story. Although she has seen UFOs, to her knowledge she has never been whisked away on such a craft or subjected to the type of frightening examinations inside a craft that abductees typically describe. Her encounters are with beings capable of moving between physical and non-physical forms, and these encounters continue to the present.

She describes them as about three feet tall, similar to the so-called Grays, but they are tan-colored with faces that are smaller and more delicate than the descriptions of Grays. "I'm fully conscious when I interact with them and have grabbed them (not recommended), held and caressed their hands and rested my hand against them during the work. When they're physical they have color, texture, are warm to the touch and have strange odors associated with their presence that remind me of the scent of vitamin tablets." They also are capable of pulling Susan out of her body and taking her on interdimensional journeys.

One thing she has in common with other abductees are the implants that she says have been placed in various parts of her body. "I've had so many strange things inserted into my body that I don't even consider it unusual anymore." The most painful experience occurred when something was inserted deep into her right thigh.

"In my journals I described the pain as if it was plunged directly into my femur and I shot out of the bed screaming in pain and cursing at the beings at the top of my lungs. The area on my thigh was so sore that I had a limp for days after the experience. It really pissed me off. I've also had things inserted in my toes and on the right side of my rib cage, just to mention a few regions. It's just a part of the work so I don't get too concerned unless it's painful and then I threaten to stop the work. They usually come back to repair the pain after the event."

Typically, Susan lays down in bed in late morning or early afternoon. That's when her voluntary contact usually take place. To understand her experiences, we'll let Susan tell her own story through one of her journal entries. We've made minor edits for clarification and style consistency.

WED NOV 15 2017 2:30 PM

I laid down this morning around 11:00 to work with the energies and I immediately experienced the familiar but strange energy move through me, starting at my legs and moving upward and creating the shift. It starts in my right leg and moves upward, then in my left leg, upward through my core. Then something opens up at the top of my head with a distinct pressure over my crown area about four inches in diameter.

At the same time there was a pressure at the base of my spine that engulfed my upper thigh and pelvis. It's a pressure/suction vibration energy shift. There are no words to describe the intensity of the experience of the shift phenomenon. It moved through my body in many directions and opened me up with a sudden energy that moved through me like a freight train, an endless freight train that came in through the base of my spine and fill my entire body with this infinite energy.

It raced through me for so long that I was feeling as if I was going too fast and was tempted to pull out of it. During this time, I had my usual assortment of visions that include faces and places and my entire body felt lifted up. I wasn't in a trance and was fully conscious of my environment. I could hear the ticking of the wall clock and ambient sound filtering into the room from the neighbors.

But I was also aware that I was someplace else and in the presence of these beings, a dozen of them crammed together, only about 3-4 feet apart and they were spinning, all spinning, counterclockwise elegantly.

They weren't beings with a physical appearance like ours, but instead were branches of energy with perfect spheres of bright, brilliantly colored lights. I could see the outline of the spheres with branches of energy extending outward in many directions. There was colored light inside the spheres with assorted shades of blues, reds and greens and their configuration would change slightly as they speeded up and slowed down their spinning, as if opening up and closing again.

It was incredible and I just watched these beings in awe for the longest time. They were so unusual and beautiful and reminded me of a vision Greg had over ten years ago that he wrote down and drew a diagram of - like wiggly stick figures with six to eight spheres in the end of each branch of energy. Then I moved on.

The freight train energy slowed down when I was observing my surroundings and sped up and intensified when I started to move again. I felt like I was the one moving, but it was the energy moving through me. I was taken through a strange area that was drab and rust colored. I don't have the words to describe this odd place although it was very detailed and clear to me. There were strange, rust-colored objects suspended in the space all around me, like an asteroid belt with an assortment of flat, rust colored objects about 8 inches wide floating everywhere around me as I was moving through the area. It was well lit but far too alien of an environment for me to feel comfortable exploring so I said no, no, I don't like being here so I'm going to pull back and put on the brakes. The energy was still rushing like a like fire hose through me from the bottom up.

I know there isn't a physical threat to me in places like this but it's important for me to maintain my emotional body so if a place is at all questionable I pull the plug and return. One type of energy moves over me in a way that causes all of my muscles to relax. I love when this wonderful wave of energy moves from the forehead down and it immediately washes away all tension I'm holding in my body.

Susan's story is astonishing because of the frequency of contact and its peculiar nature. Clearly, she isn't dealing with entities that exist in physical reality in the same sense that we do. She describes the beings in terms of quantum physics. "The beings I work with exist primarily in a wave state and we, as humans, exist as particles. They've been teaching me to exist partially in a wave state and they have learned to exist partially in a particle state."

Mainstream science and the media generally dismiss the alien contact phenomenon as non-existent, as simple fantasies and dreams, visions based on stories we've read, heard or seen. But when you take a closer look, it becomes apparent that something unusual is going on that stretches our sense of reality, and the very definition of what is real. We agree with those who say that the UFO/alien encounter phenomenon is the mystery of our time, and possibly the greatest mystery of all time.

11

CREATE YOUR VISIONS

"There is no universe without perception.
Consciousness and the cosmos are correlative.
They are one and the same."
—Robert Lanza, M.D.

Nearly two decades into the twenty-first century, more and more people are accepting the reality of paranormal experiences, according to the polls. While mainstream science and skeptics argue that you shouldn't trust your own experiences related to the paranormal, it's those personal encounters that turn people into believers. Meanwhile, more and more scientists, through their research and own experiences, are endorsing the validity of visions, of phenomena. Even taboo subjects such as UFOs and alien encounters are on the table for consideration.

The power of the Internet and social media, websites and blogs, online magazines, and podcasts, have made it easy to connect with others worldwide who have experienced what you have. Fear of ridicule is a fading anachronism of the past.

A Google search for "radio shows and podcasts that focus on the paranormal" returned nearly forty-two million links. A search for "websites, blogs, and online magazines about the paranormal" delivers more than eight million links. When you limit the search to "UFOs," the hits for radio shows and podcasts is about three-and-a-half million. If you simply Google "synchronicity," more than eight million links come up. All told, Google delivers sixty-plus million links for the types of experiences included in this book.

That's a lot of company! Maybe some of those millions have only experienced hunches or dreams that seemed to presage a future event or a powerful synchronicity that seized their attention. But they're open-minded and interested in these events and experiences.

This growing collective curiosity and fascination with the mysterious and unknown is everywhere in popular culture. TV shows like *Stranger Things* to *Travelers, Timeless, Dark,* and *Project Blue Book* reflect the notion that reality is vastly different from what we've been taught. Movies like *The Matrix, 12 Monkeys, Inception, Get Out* and *Us* carry these ideas about the paranormal into even newer and stranger territory that compel us to speculate about *what-ifs.*

What if, as the Many Worlds Theory contends, there are worlds that spin off from every decision we make? Suppose there's a version of you living a life where you didn't marry your current spouse? Where you had three kids? Where your mother didn't die from complications of Alzheimer's?

What if it's possible to cure cancer and other diseases through the focus of our minds and emotions?

What if there are people who can move objects with their minds, see into the future, feel planetary or manmade disasters hours, days or even weeks before they occur?

It begins to sound as if we're all living in a Stephen King novel, where nothing is the way it should be, the way we were taught.

Perhaps the true nature of what it means to be human is found in these *what-if* scenarios, where a new paradigm intends to be born regardless of the way the old paradigm pushes against it, criticizes and ridicules.

Throughout history, people have been guided by visions, trances, dreams, spirit contact. Mystical experiences are about journeys beyond our physical limitations, beyond the everyday world, journeys in which we recognize the interconnectedness of all things, and come away with a sense of peace and universal love, an awareness of a guiding force, a sense of being changed. Even though our culture seems permeated with polarizing points of view, at a deeper level we are all interconnected, manifested from the same Genie bottle of consciousness.

We all have psychic abilities to one degree or another. We are more than just our physical bodies. We can tap into a collective soup of knowledge and wisdom that expands who we are and what we can do. We aren't all Marvel super heroes, but the potential exists in each and every one of us to become more than who we currently are.

RESOURCES

INTRODUCTION

Roberts, Jane, *Seth Speaks: The Eternal Validity of the Soul*, Amber-Allen Publishing, 1972,
Talbot, Michael, The Holographic Universe: The Revolutionary Theory of Reality, Harper Perennial, 1991

CHAPTER 1

Sacks, Oliver, *Hallucinations*, Vintage, 2013.

Huxley, Aldous, *Doors of Perception and Heaven and Hell*, Harper Perennial Modern Classics, 2009.

Snow, Chet and Wambach, Helen, *Mass Dreams of the Future*, McGraw-Hill, 1989.

Edgar Cayce readings: https://www.edgarcayce.org/the-readings/his-readings/

CHAPTER 2

Swann, Ingo, Your Nostradamus Factor: Accessing Your Innate Ability to See into the Future, Fireside, 1993.

Jung, Carl & Basilides, *The Seven Sermons to the Dead*, Amazon Digital Services, 2013.

Jung, C.G. & Jaffe Aniela, Memories, Dreams, Reflections, Vintage, 1989.

CHAPTER 3

Sheldrake, Rupert, The Sense of Being Stared At and Other Unexplained Powers of the Human Mind: And other Unexplained Powers of the Human Mind, Park Street Press, 2013.

Miller, Arthur I, *Deciphering the Cosmic Number: The Strange Friendship of*

Wolfgang Pauli and Carl Jung, W.W. Norton & Co., 2009.

Kripal, Jeffrey R, Mutants and Mystics: Science Fiction, Superhero Comics, and the Paranormal, University of Chicago Press, 2011.

Wilhelm, Richard, The I Ching or Book of Changes, Princeton University Press, 1977.

CHAPTER 4

McTaggart, Lynn, The Intention Experiment: Using Your Thoughts to Change Your Life and the World, Atria, 2007.

McMoneagle, Joe, Mind Trek, Exploring Consciousness, Time, and Space Through Remote Viewing, Hampton Roads Publishing, 1993.

Beitman, Bernard, *Connecting with Coincidence: The New Science for Using Synchronicity and Serendipity in Your Life*, Health Communications, Inc., 2017.

Dorsey, Larry, *The Power of Premonitions*, Hay House, 2009.

Hopcke, Robert, *There are No Accidents: Synchronicities and the Stories Of Our Lives*, Riverhead Books, 1998.

Roberts, Jane, The Individual and the Nature of Mass Events, Bantam, 1982.

CHAPTER 5

Talbot, Michael, *Beyond the Quantum*, New York, Bantam, 1988.

Kean, Leslie, *Surviving Death: A Journalist Investigates Evidence for an Afterlife*, Crown 2017.

Vieira, Waldo, *Projections of the Consciousness: A Diary of Out-of-Body Experiences*, International Academy of Consciousness, 2007.

Rogo, D. Scott, *Leaving the Body: A Complete Guide to Astral Projection*, Prentice-Hall, 1983.

Black, David, *EKSTASY: Out-of-Body Experiences*, Bobbs-Merrill Company, 1975.

Taylor, Albert, *Soul Traveler: A Guide to Out-of Body Experiences and the Wonders Beyond*, Berkeley, 2000.

The story of the marathon runner was originally published here: Alvarado, C.S. (2000). Out-of-body experiences. In E. Cardeña, S.J. Lynn, & S. Krippner (Eds.), Varieties of Anomalous experience, 183—218. Washington, DC: American Psychological Association, 2000, p. 184. Alvarado talks about other cases of active OBEs at this site: https://carlossalvarado.wordpress.com/2016/05/10/out-of-body-experiences-and-physical-activity/

https://www.thedailybeast.com/uk-police-advise-officers-dont-discount-psychics-and-witches-in-investigations

https://www.medicalnewstoday.com/articles/318464.php

https://psi-encyclopedia.spr.ac.uk/articles/
out-body-experience-obe#footnote42_gq18g9t
https://www.thevibrationstate.com/methods.html
https://carlossalvarado.wordpress.com/2016/05/10/
out-of-body-experiences-and-physical-activity/

CHAPTER 6

Renier, Noreen, A Mind for Murder, Hampton Roads, 2008.
Chapter 7
Harner, Michael, *Cave and Cosmos: Shamanic Encounters with Another Reality*, North Atlantic Books, 2013.

Barnum, Barbara Stevens, *Spirituality in Nursing: The Challenge of Complexity*, Springer Publishing Company, 2010.

Harrell, Kelly, *Spirit Guide to Modern Shamanism: A Beginner's Map Charting an Ancient Path*, Soul Rocks Books, 2014.
Ingerman, Sandra and Wesselman, Hank, Awakening to the Spirit World: The Shamanic Path of Director Revelation, Sounds True, 2010.

CHAPTER 8

Kilpatrick, Sydney, *Edgar Cayce: The American Prophet*, Riverhead Books, 2001.

MacGregor, Rob, *Jewel in the Lotus: Meditation for Busy Minds*, Crossroad Press, 2016.
Video of three sessions of Jane Roberts speaking as Seth: https://www.youtube.com/watch?v=K6RuJ65DvJ0

Horowich, Mitch, *The Miracle Club: Turning Thoughts to Things*, Inner Traditions, 2018.

Streiber, Whitley, *The Afterlife Revolution*, Walker & Collier, Inc, 2017.
Dispenza, Joe, You Are the Placebo: Making Your Mind Matter, Hay House, 2014.

CHAPTER 9

Church, Dawson, *Mind to Matter: The Astonishing Science of How Your Brain Creates Material Reality*, Hay House, 2018.
Miller, Arthur I, Deciphering the Cosmic Number: The Strange Friendship of Wolfgang Pauli and Carl Jung, W.W. Norton & Co., 2010.

Keen, Leslie, *Surviving Death: A Journalist Investigates Evidence for an Afterlife*, New York, Crown 2017.

Vieira, Waldo, *Projections of the Consciousness: A Diary of Out-of-Body Experiences*, Rio De Janeiro, International Institute of Projectiology, 1995.

Taylor, Albert, *SOUL TRAVELER: A Guide to Out-of-Body Experiences and the Wonders Beyond*, New York, New American Library, 1996.

Monroe, Robert, Journeys Out of Body: The Classic Work on Out-of-Body Experience, New York, Broadway Books, updated version, 1992.

CHAPTER 10

Fuller, John, *The Interrupted Journey*, New York, Dell Books, 1967.

Hopkins, Budd, *Missing Time*, New York, Ballantine Books, 1988.

Mack, John, *Abduction: Human Encounters with Aliens*, New York, Scribner, 1994.

Streiber, Whitley, *Communion: A True Story*, New York, William Morrow, 2008.

Streiber, Whitley, *The Afterlife Revolution*, San Antonia, TX, Walker & Collier, 2018.

Keel, John, *The Mothman Prophecies: A True Story*, New York, Tor, 2013.

Schwarz, Berthold Eric, *UFO Dynamics: Psychiatric and Psychic Dimensions of the UFO Syndrome*, Highland City, FL, Rainbow Books, 1989.

ABOUT THE AUTHORS

Rob MacGregor is a New York Times bestselling author of twenty-one novels and nineteen non-fiction books in the New Age and self-help field. His novel Prophecy Rock won the Edgar Allan Poe Award for mystery writing. He has worked with George Lucas, Peter Benchley and Billy Dee Williams. He has researched anomalous phenomena for many of his books, including seven Indiana Jones sagas and two remote viewing novels. He resides in Florida. He also teaches yoga classes and leads meditation workshops.

Trish MacGregor is the author of 43 novels and numerous non-fiction books on synchronicity, astrology, the tarot, dreams. She won the Edgar Allan Poe Award for her novel Out of Sight. She and Rob co-authored the Sydney Omarr series of astrology books for ten years. Trish also teaches workshops on astrology and tarot. She lives in Florida.

Curious about other Crossroad Press books?
Stop by our site:
http://store.crossroadpress.com
We offer quality writing
in digital, audio, and print formats.

Enter the code FIRSTBOOK
to get 20% off your first order from our store!
Stop by today!

Made in the USA
Middletown, DE
26 January 2020